VGM Opportunities Seri

MW01042078

OPPORTUNITIES IN
NONPROFIT
ORGANIZATION
CAREERS

Adrian A. Paradis

Foreword by
Elaine L. Chao
President
United Way of America

6/97

VGM Career Horizons
a division of *NTC Publishing Group*
Lincolnwood, Illinois USA

Cover Photo Credits:

Clockwise from top left: Girl Scouts of the U. S. A.;
Preferred Stock; Rotary International; Preferred Stock.

Library of Congress Cataloging-in-Publication Data

Paradis, Adrian A.
    Opportunities in nonprofit organization careers / Adrian A.
    Paradis.
        p.   cm. — (VGM opportunities series)
    Includes bibliographical references.
    ISBN 0-8442-4088-5. — ISBN 0-8442-4089-3 (pbk.)
    1. Nonprofit organizations—Vocational guidance—United States.
I. Title II. Series.
HD2769.2.U6P37   1993
331.7′02—dc20   93-4667
                                                            CIP

1996 Printing

Published by VGM Career Horizons, a division of NTC Publishing Group.
© 1994 by NTC Publishing Group, 4255 West Touhy Avenue,
Lincolnwood (Chicago), Illinois 60646-1975 U.S.A.
Manufactured in the United States of America.

    6 7 8 9 0 VP 9 8 7 6 5 4 3 2

ABOUT THE AUTHOR

Adrian A. Paradis was born in Brooklyn, New York, attended schools there, majored in English at college, and later earned a B.S. degree in library service. Since then he has had a variety of business and literary experience ranging from librarian, literary critic, writer, editor, and publisher to private secretary, hotel manager, accountant, office manager, and corporate executive. The author of more than fifty books, he has written extensively in the field of vocational guidance. Mr. Paradis is married and has three children and five grandchildren; he lives in Sugar Hill, in New Hampshire's White Mountains, where he often enjoys hiking and taking motor trips.

FOREWORD

The need to help and care for one another is as old as the first human communities—and equally valid for a modern mass society. On the threshold of the twenty-first century, the nonprofit sector of the American economy is more important than ever. For many it embodies the best and most powerful values of our nation: pride in the dignity of work, the chance to put into practice an ethic of caring, and the realization that one person can make a difference.

That is why there is such a particular need for this book. *Opportunities in Nonprofit Careers* presents a broad range of material about the nonprofit community that will serve as a definitive guide for those exploring careers in the field. As this book so admirably demonstrates, the nonprofit world is wide and varied, and each chapter is enriched by concrete examples of actual professional experiences. Some of the information may surprise you, and some is common knowledge—but all of it is honest, revealing, and instructive and will be a valuable tool for individuals of any age considering a career change or aspiring to get started in this rewarding sector of the workplace.

I believe it is vital to cultivate bright, articulate, and committed men and women willing to share not only their good will and their spirit but their skills and their leadership in nonprofit enterprises.

In these times of so much change and social unrest, we must renew a sense of caring, encouraging all Americans to not only assert their rights but fulfill their duty to give something back for the common good.

It is my hope that *Opportunities in Nonprofit Careers* will help persuade a new generation to build their careers in service to this common good, embracing the opportunities that nonprofits offer for unsurpassed personal and professional growth.

Elaine L. Chao
President, United Way of America

PREFACE

Job opportunities in the nonprofit field are so diverse and numerous that it is impossible to cover all of them thoroughly, but we have tried to mention the most important. Organizations such as libraries, medical facilities, and social service agencies, for example, serve the public directly and require a broad range of skilled and nonskilled employees. However, other organizations or associations, which represent groups of people, specialists, or societies, usually require a smaller office or clerical staff plus a few trained professionals in that field. Therefore, you will find tremendous variety in the activities described in this book.

Because fund-raising is so important to nonprofit organizations, which must seek outside financial support to survive, we asked a veteran fund-raising professional to contribute a chapter about this vital subject. We recommend you give this activity serious consideration.

We hope the suggested readings in the appendices will provide you with the detailed information you will need to make a decision about your career future. This book will suggest the opportunities that exist in the nonprofit field, but you will want to read further about those areas that interest you.

CONTENTS

CHAPTER 1

THE JOBS

Rhoda Carter, director of the Mid-County Home Health Agency, greeted us in the reception room. Dressed in a trim white uniform, she looked every inch a professional. Following the usual introductions, she sat next to us and suggested that before we start our tour of the staff, she give us some background on the agency.

"First I should tell you that in the case of most nonprofit groups like ours there is a board of trustees which oversees the operation. The board does not become involved in the day-to-day business of the agency but hires the officers who may include the executive director, president, treasurer, and secretary, each of whom in turn selects members of his or her staff. The officers and also the public relations and fund-raising directors may have direct contact with the trustees and, therefore, need both personality and style to work comfortably with these people. Trustees donate their time, usually have other full-time jobs, and may be demanding. In our case each of the trustees represents a town we serve, and you may be sure that he or she will make certain we are doing a good job in that locality!

"Our trained health providers, who comprise most of our staff, bring high-quality health care and support services into people's homes whether it is for the long- or short-term. These providers are trained nurses, homemaker health aides, occupational and physical therapists, and speech pathologists. In addition to these twenty employees who work with patients, we have nine employees on our support staff here in the office. Our agency serves eleven towns, and we receive most of our support from contributions, Medicaid and Medicare payments, and regular fees." She paused, then nodded toward the receptionist whose desk was close to the front door. "Let's start our tour right here with Cindy Halstead."

RECEPTIONIST

"Cindy," Mrs. Carter called, "these folks are here to learn something about the administrative staff of a nonprofit organization. Although we're in the health care business, we need many of the same office skills as every other nonprofit association. Would you tell them briefly about your job?"

"Certainly," the young girl replied. "I'm keen about this job because I meet so many interesting men and women and there's never a dull moment. When I'm not helping people who come in for information or to see someone on the staff, I run this switchboard—and that's fun, too—or I'm busy working on whatever reports, schedules, documents, or letters staff members need typed." She hesitated. "Oh, I forgot, I open and sort all the mail each morning, too. That gives me a pretty good picture of what's going on."

Mrs. Carter explained that a volunteer comes in to relieve Cindy at lunchtime and during her vacation. "Some agencies rely on volunteers for this position," she said, "but Cindy's an excellent typist, so we prefer this arrangement. You see, she really does three jobs—reception, switchboard, and typing!"

Most receptionists are expected to know how to operate a switchboard and type, skills that can be learned in many high school commercial courses or in a postgraduate vocational/technical school. In some offices receptionists use automated office equipment such as personal computers, word processors, fax machines, and copiers. Job duties vary from office to office, but the more skills you can offer, the better your employment and salary prospects.

SECRETARY

We stepped into a long hallway and turned right to enter Mrs. Carter's office. A woman sat behind a desk in one corner of the room.

"This is my office," Mrs. Carter told us, "and that is my secretary, Hester Rollins. She's the one who handled all the arrangements for your visit. Actually, Hester is the reason this office is so efficient.

"I don't see how she does it," Mrs. Carter continued. "She's really my assistant, which means she answers my phone, prepares replies to routine inquiries for my signature, takes and transcribes dictation, does all the filing, schedules my appointments, gives information to callers, and runs occasional errands for me." She frowned. "What have I forgotten, Hester?"

Hester laughed. "My most important duty is to remind you to go to lunch or get it for you. Otherwise you'd never eat!"

Hester then told us that she had gone to secretarial school after graduating from high school and that her first job had been that of stenographer—one who takes dictation and types but does not take on secretarial responsibilities. Experience in that assignment qualified her to apply to the Mid-County Home Health Agency when there was an opening in Mrs. Carter's office.

"This is a super job," she said. "There are so many challenges because I try in every way I can to make certain Mrs. Carter isn't bothered with any of the office details."

"And I never am!" the director asserted firmly.

COMPUTER PROGRAMMER

When she put her hand on the doorknob of the next office, Mrs. Carter confessed, "This is one job I can't explain. I'm a health specialist, not a computer expert. I leave that all to Tom Daly."

As we entered, Tom was leaning over his desk staring at a small screen displaying many numbers. He looked up, then rose quickly. "Greetings to the land of computers," he said.

Mrs. Carter introduced us, then asked Tom to briefly explain what his job entailed.

"I think I can make it simple," he said. "As a programmer I prepare specific programs for the computer so that each member of the staff can make maximum use of it. Essentially my job is to write precise instructions—say, for payroll or the Medicare billing clerk—breaking down each step a staff member must take and then arranging the steps in a logical sequence that the computer can follow. I code the instructions for the computer, and each staff member follows the instructions on the screen when they enter information or need to query the computer to obtain data." He explained that each staff member has a work station with a keyboard and monitor like his to use when they enter or request information. We noted that the keyboard resembled that of any standard typewriter, which would make it easy for anyone familiar with the touch system to use.

"We could never run this agency without Tom and this computer," Mrs. Carter observed. "What with all the complicated

Medicare and Medicaid billing, to say nothing of the payroll, Tom is indispensable to our operation."

Tom then told us that computer programming—and other computer jobs—are taught in private and public vocational/technical schools, community and junior colleges, and universities. Introductory courses may be available at your high school, but you will find that a number of programmers are college graduates who also have extensive knowledge in some other business field (accounting, payroll, or inventory, for example) and thereby are more valuable to prospective employers. A college degree is not a must, but it will pay off eventually.

The *Occupational Outlook Handbook* has this to say about programmers:

> When hiring programmers, employers look for people who can think logically and who are capable of exacting analytical work. The ability to work with abstract concepts and do technical analysis is especially important for systems programmers because they work with the software that controls the computer's operation. The job calls for patience, persistence, and the ability to work with extreme accuracy, even under pressure. Ingenuity and imagination are particularly important when programmers work in areas like computer-aided design where creativity is the key.

GENERAL OFFICE CLERK

Our next stop was at the office of Elaine Prosser, who title was General Office Clerk. "Here's our 'Jack-of-all-trades,' " Mrs. Carter announced as she introduced Ms. Prosser. "Could you please give these folks a brief rundown of what you do?"

Elaine laughed. " 'Everything' would best describe my job responsibilities," she replied. "But seriously, you might say I fill in whenever someone is needed to help with a job. One morning I may be with Rich Taylor, our treasurer, working on the month-end accounting. Another day I might be asked to assist with the payroll or with scheduling the nurses. Typing, filing, running the copy machine, or even taking the mail to the post office can be part of the day's work. One of my regular duties is to order office supplies and keep an inventory of everything we must have on hand for the health team."

Mrs. Carter thanked her and led us up the hall to the next office.

TREASURER-CONTROLLER

"This is Rich Taylor, our treasurer," Mrs. Carter told us, introducing a man whose serious expression and black-rimmed glasses seemed to fit his financial responsibilities. "Next to our health care department, this is probably the most important division," she said. "Rich, can you please describe what it is a treasurer does?"

Rich then explained that every treasurer has two main functions: to receive money and spend it. The number of departmental employees depends on the size of the organization and the complexity of its operation. "Ours is a fairly small health center," he said. "Our income comes principally from the government Medicare and Medicaid payments, insurance remittances, and allotments from the towns, as well as foundation grants and individual gifts. Our accounts receivable manager handles this end of our business, accounting for all of our income. However, two employees are needed to pay our obligations. A manager of disbursements takes care of paying all the bills (accounts payable) except for payroll, which is the responsibility of a separate manager.

"This is most complicated work. Our health staff is paid by the hour and some of those employees may not work a full week. In addition to their pay, they receive mileage allotments to cover driving expenses because our health aides do all their work in the patients' homes. Then, of course, we are required by law to withhold federal and state income tax as well as the social security tax. All money withheld must be paid to the government quarterly, accompanied by detailed reports. In a large organization there may be a manager and several payroll clerks who work under his or her direction."

Rich turned and pointed to a desk in the corner of the room. "That's where John Meekings, our controller, works. His job is to prepare financial reports, oversee the accounting and budgeting process, and make audits from time to time. One of his most important duties is to keep abreast of government regulations regarding payments for visits made to patients who are on Medicare or Medicaid. You see, he's sort of a watchdog.

"I should point out that some nonprofit organizations like museums run mail order businesses and gift shops in order to raise extra funds. These activities call for other financial specialists, as well as clerks to stand behind the counters to sell the merchandise and employees to fill mail orders. Then there are the private schools, colleges, and universities, which may have huge financial departments. Just consider the money pouring in and out of a university that has several thousand students, a large faculty, and a sizable maintenance and custodial staff to care for the several buildings. You can see that the opportunities for financial specialists are extensive."

"What training do you suggest for someone interested in pursuing a career in finance?" we asked.

"I'd say a bachelor's degree in finance or accounting or, better still, a degree in business administration with emphasis on finance or accounting—or both," replied Rich.

"But what about the high school graduate who cannot go to college full time?"

"There's no reason he or she cannot take accounting and business courses at night in a community college or a vocational /technical school. Obviously such a person would have to start in a low paying position, but with further education he or she can earn promotions and should enjoy a satisfactory and well-paying career. Remember," Rich added, "if a person is really determined to do something, it is usually possible to achieve that goal, provided he or she has the necessary ability."

MANAGER OF THE FILING DEPARTMENT

Mrs. Carter next led us to the filing department, Joan Black's responsibility. We crowded into a large room, which was jammed with filing cabinets on all sides. Joan's desk, placed in the middle of the room, enabled her to reach all of the files with a minimum of walking.

As Joan talked about her position, we learned the sad fact that many high school graduates cannot remember the proper order of the twenty-six letters in the alphabet. In addition to this simple skill, a file clerk should be able to examine letters and documents and file them correctly according to subject matter, the alphabet, or a numerical system, depending on how the files are organized. When correspondence or records are requested, the file clerk finds them, gives them to the borrower, and makes a record of the loan.

"From time to time I check through the files to make certain they are in the proper order, transfer inactive files to dead storage in the basement, and destroy those letters, documents, and records that we no longer need to keep," Joan explained. "I should mention we're going to put our records on microfilm, which will mean that instead of finding a piece of paper or a file, I will locate the document on a reel of film and put it on the viewer for the person to see. If necessary we will be able to retrieve the original document from storage. This system will give us enough extra space to place the copy and mimeograph machines in here, which I'll operate. In some offices the file clerk is also expected to type, open and sort mail, and do word processing."

In response to our query regarding job qualifications, Joan said that many file clerks start out as an assistant in a filing department or may take over a filing position after a week or two of on-the-job training. Those applicants who have secretarial or typing skills and know how to operate office equipment will find better opportunities than individuals with less experience.

MANAGER OF PUBLIC RELATIONS

Harold Olsen, manager of public relations, greeted us warmly and asked us to take seats. The well-dressed young man immediately explained the purpose of public relations.

"In its very broadest sense," he said, "you might say that public relations is dealing successfully with people. However, we should further explain this statement by saying that public relations is dealing successfully with people with the emphasis on an activity that not only is beneficial to the public—such as our home health agency—but also endeavors to gain the good will and understanding of the public. Of course, every public relations program is motivated by a selfish desire to accomplish some purpose. In our case it is, frankly, our desire to establish a good reputation for rendering excellent health care and thereby gain the community's backing and financial support, which we need if we hope to keep our doors open.

"In a small operation like ours, one person can handle the job, but you will find public relations staffs of varying sizes in numerous organizations. To give you some idea of what a public relations manager does, let me quickly describe my principal activities."

He then told us how he occasionally calls upon the first selectperson of each town to thank him or her for the town's support, report how many nursing calls were made to residents of that area, and ask if there are any ways the agency can improve its services. From time to time he visits with various community leaders to report on agency activities and solicit comments or suggestions. About every two months he sends to newspapers in the area a press release describing a new agency service, introducing a new employee, or providing news about some new health program or innovation.

"When we receive a complaint through a telephone call or letter, I contact that person and try to restore his or her confidence in us. Probably my most important responsibility is to make certain that every agency employee does his or her best to make a good impression on each patient we serve, as well as on the communities in which we operate. This calls for endless vigilance and lots of new ideas, all designed to help us deal successfully with people."

Today most public relations practitioners have had previous experience as a journalist or obtained a bachelor's or master's degree in public relations or journalism.

FUND-RAISER

When Harold finished, Mrs. Carter thanked him and nodded toward an empty desk. "That's where Polly Morgan, our fund-raiser, works. Right now, she's out meeting with the officials of two philantrophic foundations that give us generous annual support. She keeps in close touch with them as well as with the budget chairperson of each town that votes funds for us. In addition she runs an annual antiques auction, which raises money for the agency, and she conducts a fund-raising campaign by mail. Like many fund-raisers she has a background in public relations, although that is not an essential qualification for the job." (See chapter 11 for more information on fund-raising.)

As we made our way back to the reception room, Mrs. Carter told us that two other nonoffice, but nevertheless important, staff members were the maintenance manager and the custodian.

"The former is responsible for making necessary repairs to the building and seeing to it that all essential service equipment, such a air-conditioning, heat, and hot water, are operating at all times. He calls in outside help if he cannot make a repair, and it is up to him to decide when painting and other routine maintenance should be performed.

"The custodian cleans our offices, rest rooms, lunch room, corridors, and other areas; removes the trash; and is available when a staff member requires help in moving or lifting furniture. He also cuts the grass, weeds flower beds, and in winter shovels the sidewalks and steps. During the summer he helps the maintenance manager with painting and other routine jobs. I need not tell you how many of these workers are employed by large educational institutions as well as other organizations that own and operate one or more buildings of their own."

After we had returned to the reception room, thanked Mrs. Carter, and were about to leave, she summarized our visit as follows: "I dare say our agency's administrative staff is quite similar to those you will find in the majority of nonprofit organizations, and a miniature copy of the larger ones. Whenever a receptionist, secretary, typist, file clerk, treasurer, or other office worker applies for a job, he or she must bring the basic skills needed for that position. It is merely a matter of applying these abilities to the organization's job requirements, which usually can be learned within a short time. As the nonprofit field continues to grow, I see increased opportunities for those who take the time and trouble to obtain the necessary training in their chosen occupation."

SELECTED AVERAGE ANNUAL EARNINGS

Billing clerks—$16,100
Bookkeeping, accounting, auditing clerks—$17,600
Clerical supervisors—$25,800
Computer operators—$19,400
Data-entry keyers—$16,700
File clerks—$14,700
Library assistants—$14,600
Mail clerks—(median weekly earnings) $300
Order clerks—$21,000
Payroll, timekeeping clerks—$19,100
Personnel clerks—$18,500
Public relations managers—$41,400 (lowest ten percent earned $20,300 or less)
Receptionists—(median weekly earnings) $270
Secretaries—$24,000
Stenographers—$21,100
Telephone operators—$16,600
Typists—$16,700
Word processors—$16,700

CHAPTER 2

CAREERS IN ASSOCIATIONS

If you are looking for a career in office work, administration, advertising, financial planning, government relations, marketing, publications, or public relations, take a good look at the job possibilities with one of the thousands of business, trade, and professional associations. Although many associations may be incorporated, making money is not their goal. Service is the object, because the members (whether individuals or companies) of the associations have banded together to achieve common goals and solutions to common problems.

Associations vary in size, from one that may have a few members like the Association of Management Consulting Firms with fifty members, to the giant American Association of Retired Persons with more than 30,000,000 members, or the National Wildlife Federation with 5,000,000 members, or the National Education Association with more than 2,000,000 members. There are even associations such as the American Federation of Processing Societies whose members include societies of computer professionals and associations of computer businesses. More than a million men and women work for associations, a good field for those seeking career opportunities.

Note that many associations are concentrated in four cities: Chicago, Los Angeles, New York, and Washington, DC. You may also find a job in one of the state or local associations that usually are located in state capitals. Many associations headquartered outside the nation's capital have offices in the District of Columbia.

GOVERNMENT RELATIONS

Mark Randall, executive director of an association of manufacturers, was seated behind his massive desk. Looking through the windows to his left, we could see the Washington Monument looming in the distance.

"There's nothing mysterious about my job," he was saying. "We represent about fifty medium-sized manufacturing companies. Essentially our responsibility is to make information about our industry available to everyone who contacts us for data of one kind or another. At the same time our members call upon us for all types of help such as obtaining the text of a proposed Senate bill, the name of a congressional committee chairperson, duty charged on imported steel bars, a copy of a hard-to-get government publication, current salary statistics for purchasing directors, and numerous other requests.

LOBBYING

"What about lobbying?" we asked. "Aren't most Washington-based associations involved in this activity?"

"Like other organizations we direct our lobbying efforts to the Congress, especially the committees that draft laws, the executive departments, and the regulatory agencies that make the rules our industry must obey. Sometimes at the request of a member of Congress, we offer testimony to committees. We often supply

Congress or a regulatory agency with detailed information related to pending legislation, or even help by submitting drafts of bills suitable to be incorporated into legislation or rule-making. In return, government officials call upon us for information and help in doing their job. Thus it's a two-way street."

Mr. Randall said that he had two "government relations" employees who work "up on the hill." They become acquainted with key government officials to whom they make their members' views known regarding proposed bills and regulations. They also monitor what is going on in the government from day to day and report back to the members on all matters of interest to them.

"The public in general seems to take a pretty dim view of lobbyists," we observed. "Do you think this is fair or accurate?"

Mr. Randall smiled. "I'm a registered lobbyist, and I'm not ashamed of my profession," he replied. "I see my role as one of informing government people, helping them, and working with them when called upon. In other words this organization tries to give impartial service to every branch of government. Sure there are always a few rotten apples in every barrel, but I would say the majority of the lobbyists I know are not guilty of wrongdoing. I would certainly encourage any young person who seeks a fascinating and highly useful career to consider preparing for a job like mine." He paused, then added, "But remember, this isn't all an association does.

"Before you leave, just let me put in a word for the members of our office staff—the receptionists, secretaries, clerical workers, computer experts, and all the others without whom no association could function. There's a host of interesting job opportunities in these positions.

"I'd also like to point out that in small or medium-sized associations like ours, where a department may have two or three functions, an employee would have to perform duties in more than one area, which adds to his or her job experience. In larger organizations, departments have a single function, and staff members are responsible only for this one activity."

ASSOCIATION EXECUTIVE PERSONNEL

To give you an overall idea of the wide scope of most association work and the administrative positions to which you might aspire, here are brief job descriptions as outlined in the *Occupational Outlook Quarterly,* Spring 1983:

Chief paid executive. Serves as the top administrative and executive official; responsible for overall administration and operation of headquarters and field activities.

Deputy chief paid executive. Serves as full-time number-two person on the staff.

Director of administration. Handles internal administrative matters of the association.

Advertising director. Develops and administers the association's national, regional, and/or local advertising activities.

Chief staff attorney. Serves as full-time head of the association's legal staff to handle legal matters pertaining to association activities.

Chief economist. Serves as the chief employee in charge of economic analyses and economic research pertaining to the association's programs and activities.

Communications director. Directs all communications activities including public relations, media relations, membership communications, and all association publications.

Controller. Directs the financial affairs of the association.

Convention and meetings director. Manages the conventions and other meetings, books space, hires and directs service contractors, arranges and coordinates all activities at the meeting site.

Education director. Develops and administers the members' and/or public educational programs of the association.

Field staff director. Supervises the association's field staff and visits field staff offices to meet with personnel.

Government relations officer. Develops and guides the association's legislative program; keeps informed on laws affecting association members; maintains contracts with legislative and other governmental agencies on matters of association interest.

Institute director. Directs the association's training school or educational institute for instruction of members.

Marketing director. Develops and guides marketing program; provides assistance to members in developing markets for the industry.

Member services director. Develops and administers the association's programs for member services.

Membership director. Directs and administers the association's program to attract new members.

Publication editor. Edits association's principal publications; directs staff responsible for preparation and issuance of all publications issued by the association.

Public relations director. Directs the association's promotions, publicity, and public relations programs; provides public relations assistance to members and member committees.

Regional office manager. Directs the activities of the association in a certain area or region of the country, supervising and administering the staff of the regional office.

Research director. Directs the association's technical research activities; assists members develop and execute their own technical research programs.

Secretary. Serves as chief staff person in charge of official association records; maintains minutes of board and committee meetings; serves as secretary to the board of directors and/or the executive committee.

Technical director. Plans and administers the technical activities of the association; assists members in developing and executing their own technical programs.

Treasurer. Serves as full-time staff person in charge of treasury matters; has overall responsibility for safeguarding the association's financial resources.

Head, Washington office. For associations headquartered outside Washington, DC, serves as the governmental liaison official in Washington; keeps informed on pending legislation and regulations; presents association's point of view on behalf of the membership; advises and assists members on federal regulatory and legislative matters.

Staff assistants support many of the positions described above. Numerous entry-level positions are found in editorial and public relations work, membership services, promotion, and planning of conventions and meetings. Typing skills are generally expected of entry-level candidates. No special degree is usually required, although you will find that if you take courses in finance, marketing, management, and journalism, they will prove helpful. Some colleges offer courses in association management, and the American Society of Association Executives provides continuing education courses and seminars in association management.

Some association professionals have heavy travel schedules and make wide contacts, which can lead to other employment opportunities. Association employees often move over to private industry or government service, and on the other hand, capable people in government and industry frequently transfer to association work.

A good way to find out whether a career in this field might be for you is to volunteer to work for a group in which you hold membership. You could do this during the summer for a month or two. If this is not possible, an entry-level position will give you good exposure to the pros and cons of working for an association.

Salaries for workers in associations can be low, with entry-level positions paying $12,000 to $15,000 annually. With experience you can work up to better paying jobs, and as you develop qualifications in one or more fields of association work, your earnings potential should also grow. Salaries for director staff positions may range from $25,000 to $60,000.

For further information, contact the American Society of Association Executives, 1575 Eye Street, NW, Washington, DC 20005.

CHAPTER 3

BUSINESS-RELATED ORGANIZATIONS

CHAMBERS OF COMMERCE

Rod McCarthy, the executive director of the Pine Haven Chamber of Commerce, sat up straight behind his desk. Dressed in the informal fashion of the Southwest, he was wearing a brown slack suit and fancy leather boots. A friendly smile greeted us as we settled into the couch opposite him.

"What can I do for you?" he asked.

"We're interested in learning something about career opportunities in a chamber of commerce," we replied. "As a starter, what do you see as the purpose of your chamber?"

"We see our job here as one that is dedicated to improving the community." He paused for a moment and then continued. "Perhaps our most important job is bringing new industry to town. Just yesterday I returned from Chicago where I've been trying to persuade an electronics firm to move their plant here to Pine Haven. Been there several times and finally they decided to make the change. That will mean seventy-two jobs in town and thousands in added tax revenues." He smiled, nodded his head, and then went on. "But our purpose isn't just to bring in new industries and promote business, which many people think is all we do. Instead, we want to make Pine Haven a better place for everyone to live."

"Just how do you do that?" we asked.

"In many ways. Let me give you just a few examples."

He explained that the chamber runs a Spring Street Fair each year when merchants set up special booths on the sidewalk, and entertainers roam the streets to amuse young and old. This benefits both the merchants and the public. In the fall an art show held on Main Street affords the local artists and craftspeople opportunity to showcase their works. "It attracts outsiders to Pine Haven, and they provide an additional market for the various exhibitors. It also brings extra business to the established merchants. At the same time it creates a good feeling in the community.

"Every year or so we bring a circus to town. This is fun for all, but it also helps support the chamber. We divide some of the profits among a scholarship fund, the hospital, and the 4-H organization."

Another community service is helping representatives of major political parties arrange for public meetings to inform citizens. "Once we held a luncheon so that the governor could present an important new plan for which he needed citizen backing." A useful service the chamber offers is an information booth in the center of town. Its membership is also available to owners of new business who may need advice and introductions around the community.

"How should one prepare for a career in this field?" we asked Mr. McCarthy.

"Work in public relations provides good background, and if one has administrative experience and know-how, that's important too. Best of all is an imaginative mind that will come up with ideas for new programs. If one could find a beginning clerical or other entry position in a large city chamber, that would be one way to obtain experience and training.

"Naturally the larger the chamber the greater the number of jobs and different skills required. In a large city you might find that in addition to the executive director and administrative staff, the chamber employs specialists such as accountants, statisticians, urban planners, public relations specialists, a writer, a graphic artist, and perhaps a lobbyist or two."

"Do you suppose it would be possible to work summers for a chamber to obtain experience?" we asked.

"Possibly, but in a small town like Pine Haven where there is just a director and his secretary, you could not expect to receive a salary. Still, the experience would be valuable when you start looking for a job after graduation."

"How much might one expect to earn in the top position?"

"I'd say that the average small town chamber like ours pays in the area of $15,000 to $25,000 for a director, depending on the amount of education and experience he or she offers. In larger organizations you would expect to receive $40,000 and more. As a rule salaries are usually the largest expense of any chamber."

Mr. McCarthy rose and thanked us for coming. "Remember money isn't everything," he said as he shook hands. "The greatest satisfaction one can gain from this job is the knowledge that he or she is helping better the lives of many townspeople. No one will pin a medal on your jacket but there will be those in the community who will be aware of what you are doing and who will admire you for your efforts."

Moving east from the small Pine Haven Chamber of Commerce to the huge Chamber of Commerce of the United States in Washington, DC, we find an altogether different setting. Organized in 1912 at the urging of then President William Howard Taft, the chamber's purpose was to help "Congress keep in closer touch with commercial affairs." Today its 200,000 members consider it a major proponent for business interests.

As the "voice of business," the chamber is primarily concerned with telling members of Congress and government officials what the business community thinks about issues, pending legislation, the national economy, and other subjects that affect the nation's welfare. It also offers many diverse programs to educate and help businesspeople and prepares and publishes numerous special reports and studies. To accomplish these programs it employs economists, statisticians, political scientists, and other specialists to provide information needed by staff members who are responsible for conducting the various activities. Its best known publication is the monthly magazine, *Nation's Business,* which employs editors, writers, researchers, graphic artists, advertising salespeople, and other production specialists.

The address of your local chamber of commerce will be found in the telephone book. The Chamber of Commerce of the United States is located at 1615 H Street NW, Washington, DC 20062.

BETTER BUSINESS BUREAUS

In 1911 the National Vigilance Committee organized to help business leaders draw up and maintain standards for national advertising and to stop selling abuses. Three years later the first Better Business Bureau opened in Minneapolis to carry out the objectives of the Vigilance Committee. Almost eighty years later, there were some seven hundred local better business bureaus, all linked by the Council of Better Business Bureaus.

The principal objective of each bureau is to protect the American consumer against fraudulent or false business practices and act as the local spokesperson in the consumer field. To accomplish this, a bureau needs a staff that includes members capable of investigating business practices, uncovering fraud, and preparing cases against violators. This may call for a variety of people trained in areas such as economics, law, public relations, financial analysis, and business. The local bureaus are busy offices. During the year they handle over 3,400,000 calls from the public requesting help, information, and advice, as well as reporting abuses in the consumer field.

The Council of Better Business Bureaus has a staff of approximately one hundred. It offers comparable but broader career opportunities than the average local bureau to those interested in this field.

Addresses of local bureaus will be found in the telephone book's white pages. The Council of Better Business Bureaus is located at 4200 Wilson Boulevard, Arlington, VA 22203.

THE JAYCEES

If a chamber of commerce career intrigues you, don't overlook the Jaycees, the United States Junior Chamber of Commerce. The Jaycee creed is as follows:

> We believe: That faith in God gives meaning and purpose to human life; That the brotherhood of man transcends the sovereignty of nations; That economic justice can best be won by free men through free enterprise; That government should be of laws rather than of men; That earth's great treasure lies in human personality; And that service to humanity is the best work of life.

The organization's purpose is to provide leadership training and personal development for men and women ages twenty-one through thirty-nine. "A Jaycee organization is a constructive action organization of young persons who devote a portion of their time to community service in the public interest, developing young persons as leaders of their community . . . Three priority areas for the 1990s are the environment, drug and alcohol abuse prevention, and governmental affairs. Besides youth and family life programs, scholarships for students are provided through the War Memorial Fund."

There are approximately 4,500 chapters with some 215,000 members nationwide. For the address of a local Jaycee, see the white pages of your telephone book or write the Jaycees, P.O. Box 7, Tulsa, OK 74121–0007.

TRADE ASSOCIATIONS

A chamber of commerce consists of businesspeople representing many industries in an area, whereas all members of a trade association belong to the same industry and may be scattered throughout the country.

The late C. Jay Judkins, Chief of the Trade Association Division of the U.S. Department of Commerce from 1930–1963, defined a trade association as:

> . . . a nonprofit, cooperative, voluntarily-joined organization of business competitors designed to assist its members and its industry in dealing with mutual business problems in several of the following areas: accounting practices, business ethics, commercial and industrial research, standardization, statistics, trade promotion, and relations with the Government, employees and the general public.

Few trade associations have branches or local offices, hence job opportunities are centered at their headquarters. Here follows a selective list of some of the largest organizations:

Air Transport Association of America
  1709 New York Avenue NW
  Washington, DC 20006

American Bankers Association
  1120 Connecticut Avenue NW
  Washington, DC 20036

American Council of Life Insurance
  1001 Pennsylvania Avenue NW
  Washington, DC 20004

American Gas Association
  1515 Wilson Boulevard
  Arlington, VA 22209

Association of American Railroads
  350 F Street NW
  Washington, DC 20001

Chemical Manufacturers Association
  2501 M Street NW
  Washington, DC 20037

Credit Union National Association
  P.O. Box 431
  Madison, WI 53701

Direct Marketing Association
  11 West Forty-second Street
  New York, NY 10036

Electronic Industries Association
  1722 I Street NW
  Washington, DC 20006

Graphic Arts Technical Foundation
  4615 Forbes Avenue
  Pittsburgh, PA 15213

National Association of Manufacturers
  1331 Pennsylvania Avenue NW
  Washington, DC 20004

National Decorating Products Association
  1050 North Lindbergh Boulevard
  St. Louis, MO 63132

National Federation of Independent Business
  150 West Twentieth Avenue
  San Mateo, CA 94403

National Food Processors Association
  1401 New York Avenue NW
  Washington, DC 20005

National Retail Hardware Association
  770 North High School Road
  Indianapolis, IN 46214

National Retail Merchants Association
  100 West Thirty-first Street
  New York, NY 10001

National Rural Utilities Cooperative Finance Corporation
  1115 Thirtieth Street NW
  Washington, DC 20007

National Tooling and Machinery Association
  9300 Livingston Road
  Ft. Washington, MD 20744

Timber Operators Council
  6825 Southwest Sandburg Street
  Tigard, OR 97223

PROFESSIONAL SOCIETIES

Individuals who share a common background in a subject such as chemistry, engineering, law, medicine, retailing, or teaching form societies or associations to exchange ideas, discuss problems, establish professional standards, and expand their knowledge of the subject. Many professional societies are similar to trade associations because of their broad range of activities.

Some of the more important groups include the following:

American Bar Association
  750 North Lake Shore Drive
  Chicago, IL 60611

American Institute of Architects
  1735 New York Avenue NW
  Washington, DC 20006

American Management Association
    135 West Fiftieth Street
    New York, NY 10020

American Mathematical Society
    P.O. Box 6248
    Providence, RI 02940

American Society of Landscape Architects
    4401 Connecticut Avenue NW
    Washington, DC 20008

American Statistical Association
    1429 Duke Street
    Alexandria, VA 22314

Association for Systems Management
    24587 Bagley Road
    Cleveland, OH 44138

Professional Secretaries International
    10502 NW Ambassador Drive
    Kansas City, MO 64195

Society of Actuaries
    475 North Martingale Road
    Schaumburg, IL 60176

For a list of additional nonprofit professional societies, see the Science, Technology, and Engineering section in chapter 9.

FARM AND AGRICULTURAL ORGANIZATIONS

There are a number of farm-related organizations, some of which have regional or state offices throughout the country. Readers interested in agriculture might well investigate some of the following organizations and also review others listed in the Gale *Encyclopedia of Associations*. The American Farm Bureau Federation listing is the central office for a "grass roots" organization, this being a federation of some forty-nine state farm bureaus with 3,300,000 members on a family basis. For the address of the nearest bureau in your state, look in your telephone directory under your county or ask your public librarian for assistance.

American Farm Bureau Federation
  225 Touhy Avenue
  Park Ridge, IL 60068

American Society of Farm Managers and Rural Appraisers
  950 South Cherry Street
  Denver, CO 80222

National Farmers Organization
  720 Davis Avenue
  Corning, IA 50841

National Grange
  1616 H Street NW
  Washington, DC 20006

National Milk Producers Federation
  1840 Wilson Boulevard
  Arlington, VA 22201

STOCK EXCHANGES

The world-famous New York Stock Exchange opened for business in 1791 under a butternut tree on New York City's Wall Street to provide a place where newly formed companies could raise money by selling stock. It also enabled traders to buy and sell their shares once the stock had come onto the market. Today it is the largest exchange in the world, and there are many smaller exchanges scattered about the country.

It may surprise you that a book on nonprofit organizations includes, of all groups, associations representing stock and community exchanges, security dealers, and investment companies.

This is because these associations provide a service to their members that enables them to trade securities, and they are not intended to make a profit. Even the New York Stock Exchange recently became a nonprofit organization and now is owned by the stock brokers whose very purpose is to make money!

Brokers who belong to an exchange execute their customers' orders to buy or sell shares of stock on the exchange floor. They do this by contracting other brokers who handle the same stock, endeavoring to obtain the best possible price for their customers, and when the two brokers are in agreement, they trade.

The principal stock exchanges are nonprofit operations and, therefore, listed below. There are other smaller exchanges that do not qualify for listing in this book; your public library could probably furnish the names and addresses of these organizations.

American Stock Exchange
    86 Trinity Street
    New York, NY 10006

Midwest Stock Exchange
    One Financial Place
    440 South LaSalle Street
    Chicago, IL 60605

New York Stock Exchange
    11 Wall Street
    New York, NY 10005

Pacific Stock Exchange
    301 Pine Street
    San Francisco, CA 94104
    (There is also a branch in Los Angeles.)

THE SECURITIES INDUSTRY

Brokers and others who trade or handle stocks, bonds, options, and other forms of securities for customers are considered members of the securities industry. Although theirs are profit-making enterprises, the firms and members belong to nonprofit associations that regulate the industry and also represent it to the public and before legislative bodies. Again, if finance interests you, you might want to look into one of the following organizations, each of which offers a wide range of employment opportunities.

Investment Company Institute
    1600 M Street NW
    Washington, DC 20036

National Association of Securities Dealers
    1735 K Street NW
    Washington, DC 20006

Securities Industry Association
    120 Broadway
    New York, NY 10271

COMMODITY EXCHANGES

Commodity markets have existed for hundreds of years, originally to provide a place where farmers, woodsmen, miners, and other producers could sell their products. Today there are markets for every commodity from butter, eggs, wheat, corn, and soybeans to pork bellies, gold, silver, lumber, coffee, petroleum, etc. You can find daily quotes for many of these and other commodities in the financial section of metropolitan newspapers. They may show the current prices as well as the "futures" price, which we explain below.

Most of the commodity exchanges (some of which are known as boards of trade) listed below are located far from the producers (farmers, mining and lumber companies, etc.) who use these organizations to market their products. Producers sign contracts promising to deliver goods of a specified quality and quantity on a certain future date to whomever holds the contract at that time. Thus producers know that they will be able to sell their alfalfa, potatoes, rubbers, gold, and other products when ready for market. The individual or company who bought the contract also is assured of having the commodity at a given date and at a firm price.

Enter the speculator, an individual who hopes to make a profit by buying and selling these "future contracts" (commonly referred to as "futures"). If that individual knows the commodities business, he or she will not hold a contract with an obligation to buy a commodity at a set price on the date it is to be delivered if he or she thinks that the market price will go down before then.

Thus if you held a futures to buy a carload of eggs at 60 cents a dozen and expect the price will rise before you have to take delivery, you should be able to sell the eggs at a profit. However, if you foresee that prices may fall, you sell the contract to someone who thinks the price will rise. One of you will be wrong—and that is what speculation is all about.

A trader who may be a speculator gives buy and sell orders to a firm that is a member of a commodity exchange that maintains a market for the commodity in which the trader is interested. The buy or sell order is transmitted to the exchange trading floor where a member of the firm tries to make the best possible deal for the customer. Members of commodity firms also trade for their own account.

Here follows a listing of the principal commodity exchanges:

American Soybean Association
  P.O. Box 27300
  St. Louis, MO 63141

Board of Trade of Kansas City, Missouri
  4800 Main Street
  Kansas City, MO 64112

Chicago Mercantile Exchange
  30 South Wacker Drive
  Chicago, IL 60606

Coffee, Sugar and Cocoa Exchange
  Four World Trade Center
  New York, NY 10048

Commodity Exchange
  Four World Trade Center
  New York, NY 10048

Fort Worth Grain Exchange
  P.O. Box 4422
  Fort Worth, TX 76106

Los Angeles Grain Exchange
  2300 East Lambert Road
  La Hambra, CA 90631

Mid-America Commodity Exchange
  141 West Jackson Boulevard
  Chicago, IL 60604

National Cattlemen's Association
  P.O. Box 3469
  Englewood, CO 80155

National Corn Growers Association
  1000 Executive Parkway
  St. Louis, MO 63141

New York Cotton Exchange
  Four World Trade Center
  New York, NY 10048

New York Mercantile Exchange
  Four World Trade Center
  New York, NY 10048

U.S. Wheat Associates
  1220 L Street NW
  Washington, DC 20006

EARNINGS SUMMARY

Salary figures are not available for organizations mentioned in this chapter. However, the figures that Rod McCarthy cited for chambers of commerce (based on their size) might apply to better business bureaus and Jaycees, as well as to trade and professional societies. The stock and commodity exchanges offer greater income possibilities, and a beginning job with one of them could lead to an exciting and well-paying career!

CHAPTER 4

CULTURAL ORGANIZATIONS

LIBRARIES

Probably every reader of this book is familiar with some library, even if it is just a small collection of books in a classroom. Few readers, however, are aware of the varied and challenging career opportunities libraries offer those who prepare to enter this field. It was estimated in 1990 that there were about 150,000 librarians in the United States. School, college, and university libraries employed most of them. The rest worked in public and special libraries, while a few were consultants or administered federal and state library programs.

The once-stereotyped image of a thin spinsterish librarian has disappeared. She was thought only to have checked books in and out while maintaining strict silence in the library's reading rooms. She might have had an assistant who returned books to their proper places on the shelves and dusted the volumes. The average library offered its patrons no special services.

In contrast, today's library is an information center staffed for the most part by professionally trained men and women. It is true that even now many villages have small libraries administered by untrained but conscientious volunteers who may or may not have any assistants. However, we are not concerned here with these institutions but rather want to see what opportunities larger libraries offer.

To obtain an up-to-date picture of the contemporary library scene, we visited with a librarian who had recently retired from her position as director of a large metropolitan library system. After graduating from a leading library school, she spent her entire career in her city's public library, taking out a few years to care for her family. Her views on library work grew and changed even as the attitudes and services of libraries shifted radically.

"How would you advise a young man or woman who wants to pursue a career in library service?" we asked her.

"If at all possible he or she should obtain a liberal arts degree and then a master's in library science at a graduate school, preferably one with American Library Association, or at least state, approval. Five years of study will pay off in terms of job opportunities and earnings."

"But what do you suggest for the student who wants to enter librarianship but either cannot or does not want to spend five years in college?"

"Such an individual can either take a beginning clerical job in a library and gradually work through the ranks by obtaining training or taking courses in a community or vocational/technical school," she replied. "That person would then qualify for subprofessional positions, perhaps even rising to a supervisory post. Incidentally, many librarians have earned money and gained experience by working in clerical positions while completing their studies."

"Could you give us some idea of what a young person might expect to find in today's library?"

"That's a difficult question," she said. "You must remember that each library has a distinctive character. Although most use similar methods of arranging their collections and making library materials available, their services are imaginative and varied and form distinctive patterns. That is because an alert librarian tailors the institution's services to the community's needs. Thus a library located in a town with a large population of artists will emphasize art throughout its collection. Conversely a library in a factory town might have a good technical collection for patrons who need such information in connection with their job responsibilities or to help them advance their careers.

"You might say that all libraries lend books, but most provide services and programs that reflect the community's needs as perceived by an alert director and staff. Also, over the years libraries have responded to the requirements of their patrons by adding cassettes, CDs, videocassettes, films, and even framed reproductions of fine art. This variety is what can make librarianship so interesting and such fun!"

We asked her to tell us something about how a library is organized.

"Essentially a library is divided into two sections," she explained. "There are user services provided by those who work directly with patrons in reference, children's, or audiovisual departments, for example; and technical services provided by behind-the-scenes specialists such as catalogers, acquisition librarians, and staff who prepare materials for patrons' use."

Thus there are many library specialists, she added, a few of whom include:

Acquisition librarians, who select and order books, films, periodicals, recordings, and other materials.

Catalogers and classifiers, who classify books and other library materials by subject and describe them on cards, computer disks, or other special tools. (All libraries, large or small, general or specialized, must have staff to perform these functions.)

Academic librarians, who work in college and university libraries and serve the students, faculty, and research staff.

School librarians, who administer a library in a private or public school library, teach students how to use it, and provide inspiration to widen pupils' reading horizons.

Reference librarians, who administer the reference collection, provide quick answers to commonly asked questions, or help the user find in-depth material for his or her recreational, educational, or career needs. Some reference work is common to all libraries and departments, but many libraries have special reference departments.

Children's and young adult librarians, who select materials for children and teens, show them how to use the library, and open their eyes to the joys of reading.

Bookmobile librarians, who serve the need of rural or specialized areas usually with books from a regional or state library.

Special librarians, who work in business libraries or information centers of nonprofit organizations and foundations.

Systems librarians, who provide advisory and supplementary services to systems and networks of libraries, possibly including cataloging or interlibrary loans. (All but two states in the United States have some form of system for interlibrary cooperation.)

In a typical library the nonprofessional staff may consist of assistants with clerical and/or business skills who help with checking out books, filing, and doing whatever else may be needed. Since they are often the first person a patron meets, their skill and responsiveness is important to the image of the library. Pages in large libraries may locate books and bring them to the patrons requesting them. Custodians and maintenance workers take care of the physical premises.

A new specialist—the computer expert—is now working in many libraries. He or she is becoming an increasingly important staff member as librarians turn to computers to keep up with the information explosion that is changing traditional ways of thinking and operating. The computer specialist in a library may be trained either as a librarian or as a computer programmer, ideally as both.

For a varied and challenging career in librarianship, investigate the fascinating and rewarding positions that can be yours.

SELECTED AVERAGE ANNUAL EARNINGS

Bookmobile drivers—$14,600

Librarians—According to the *Library Journal,* average annual earnings of library school graduates ranged from $24,400 in public libraries to $26,200 in school libraries; in college and university libraries, average annual earnings were $24,000 and in special libraries $27,000.

Library technicians—$21,700 in the federal government; no figures available for nonprofit organizations.

For other positions, see the Selected Average Annual Earnings section at the conclusion of chapter 1.

For further information, contact one or more of the following organizations:

American Library Association
50 East Huron Street
Chicago, IL 60611

American Theological Library Association
St. Meinrad School of Theology
St. Meinrad, IN 47577

Medical Library Association
6 North Michigan Avenue
Chicago, IL 60602

Special Libraries Association
1700 Eighteenth Street NW
Washington, DC 20009

HISTORICAL SOCIETIES

Newspapers feed their readers a daily ration of stories revolving around murder, crime, fraud, bankruptcies, natural and man-made disasters, to say nothing of war and genocide. Little wonder many Canadians and Americans alike see scant hope for the future, both for themselves and their children.

Nevertheless, what newspapers fail to report, because it has no sensational value, is the widespread patriotism and pride in one's heritage that does exist among many men and women. This is evidenced by the strong provincial loyalty displayed in parts of Canada and the sentimental enthusiasm that supported the United States' 1976 bicentennial birthday party. Today, in numerous communities throughout both countries, citizens are involved in projects that aim to preserve their heritage before it is forgotten. If you, too, share a love and reverence for the past, you will find this a broad field of fascinating careers awaiting you once you have acquired the necessary background and training.

History is not a dead subject, as you will learn quickly whether you visit a tiny historical society run by a half-dozen dedicated volunteers or travel to one of the large city, state, or provincial societies.

"Career opportunities run the gamut of a part-time directorship of a small society to administrative head of a major institution," Brenda Francote, herself the director of a medium-sized society, told us. "Although the majority of historical societies are too small to afford even a part-time director or curator, there are many, mostly in affluent communities, that support a paid staff."

"What do historical societies do?" we asked Ms. Francote.

"The principal purpose of any historical society is to preserve and interpret the history of the locale or the specialized subject for which it was organized. This is done by collecting books, pamphlets, letters, diaries, memorabilia, pictures, in fact, anything and everything relating to yesterday that will help people visualize and understand the past. Usually this requires the staff to establish extensive files and probably a library as well. As for artifacts, furniture, and other items, many societies establish museums to exhibit this part of their collections." (See the following section for a discussion of museums.)

"Because town historical societies comprise the majority of these organizations, what kind of activities do they undertake?" we wanted to know.

Ms. Francote smiled and showed us a bulletin of the Connecticut League of Historical Societies. "This will give you some idea," she said. "One society held a flea market to raise money; another held its annual Colonial Crafts Festival; a third sponsored a tour of old houses in town. One society's annual exhibit displayed worn-out old shoes, including some from the period 1700 to 1840. There's no limit to what an imaginative person can do."

If you are interested in this type of career and are not already active in an historical organization, volunteer to assist in some capacity at your nearest society or museum so you can obtain experience and learn more about what these groups do. You will find that at the larger societies, which employ paid staffs, you may be able to gain a toehold by joining in some clerical, secretarial, or administrative capacity if you lack a college degree or professional background and training. For further information contact one or more of the following:

American Historical Association
    400 A Street SE
    Washington, DC 20003

American Association for State and Local History
    172 Second Avenue N
    Nashville, TN 37201

National Trust for Historic Preservation
    1785 Massachusetts Avenue NW
    Washington, DC 20036

Organization of American Historians
112 North Bryan Street
Bloomington, IN 47408

The American Association for State and Local History publishes a *Directory of Historical Societies in the United States and Canada.* This directory gives for each listing the size of the staff, number of members, and major programs, and it will give you a fairly good idea of its size and the scope of its operations. Your state historical society may also publish a directory of local societies.

MUSEUMS

Historical societies are not the only organizations that operate museums. Others range from New York City's famous Metropolitan Museum of Art, or the Henry Ford Dearborn Museum and Greenfield Village, to the *Arizona* Battleship Museum in Hawaii, the Barnum and Bailey Circus Museum in Sarasota, Florida, and the several museums operated by the National Park Service. There are over 6,000 museums in the United States. As for their size and variety, the museum devoted to New Hampshire's Old Man of the Mountain is housed in one room of the Franconia Town Hall and contrasts greatly with the giant Smithsonian Institution, the numerous United States' museums that comprise many research centers and museums devoted to basic research, arts, science, history, and public education. The fact that there is such a variety of museums throughout both Canada and the United States offers opportunities to match your major subject interest with one of these institutions and possibly find a career there.

It is impossible to describe the "typical museum," because each is a unique organization. That is what makes this activity so interesting and challenging. Here are the names of a few additional institutions that illustrate this point:

Illinois Railway Museum
Whaling Museum Society
Museum of Modern Art
Museum of Science and Industry
Museum of Afro-American History
Basketball Hall of Fame
American Museum in Britain
Museum of the American Indian
Museum of Comparative Zoology
Museum of Arms and Military History
Museum of Natural History
Custer Battlefield Museum

Principal museum positions include the following:

Director is the top administrative officer who oversees and directs all the museum's activities. Some museums also employ an assistant director.

Curator is a professional who has been trained in archeology, art, history, science, etc. This key employee may have numerous responsibilities, the principal ones being to plan and make all arrangements for exhibits and displays; to find, purchase, and restore, if necessary, articles to add to the museum's collection; to do research; to act in an advisory capacity; and to catalog and preserve. As in the case of the director, it is not unusual for there to be an assistant curator.

Restorer works on paintings, furniture, artifacts, memorabilia, and other objects that need to be restored.

Exhibit technician builds, assembles, and sets up exhibits and services them.

Attendant provides information and helps operate the museum. (Docents, who are usually volunteers, do teaching or instruction for museum visitors.)

In addition there may be other research associates, art conservators, teachers, maintenance personnel, security guards, custodians, and clerical and secretarial employees employed by the museums.

Your best preparation for a career in this field is a liberal arts degree. Following that, you may want to do graduate work in your chosen field. An alternative method is to complete an internship and study at the same time.

A yearly survey of the latest salary information on thirty-seven professional positions in art museums throughout the United States is published by the American Association of Museums and is available at the association's bookstore located at the address below.

For further information, contact one or more of the following organizations:

American Association of Museums
  1225 Eye Street NW
  Washington, DC 20005

American Association of Zoological Parks and Aquariums
  Route 88, Oglebay Park
  Wheeling, WV 26003

National Trust for Historical Preservation
  1785 Massachusetts Avenue NW
  Washington, DC 20036

Society of American Archivists
  600 South Federal Street
  Chicago, IL 60605

United States Department of the Interior*
  National Park Service
  Box 37126
  Washington, DC 20013

*(Museums have mostly small curator, exhibit, and museum technician staffs.)

CHAPTER 5

THE HEALTH CARE INDUSTRY

If you are like most people who enjoy good health, you have probably taken it for granted. It is only when we become sick or have an accident that requires a visit to a doctor or an enforced hospital stay that we are truly aware of the medical field. Health care is a business generating $8 billion and is one of the largest service industries in the country. It is also the largest nonprofit activity discussed in this book. It offers almost unlimited career opportunities to everyone looking for a job, and that includes those who have little or no skills or job experience to offer. Actually the greatest variety of career opportunities within the entire nonprofit sector will be found here.

According to the *Occupational Outlook Handbook:*

> Health care will continue to be one of the fastest growing industries in the economy. Employment in the health service industries is projected to grow from 8.9 to 12.8 million. Improvements in medical technology, and a growing and aging population will increase the demand for health services. Employment in home health care services—the fastest growing industry in the economy—nursing homes, and offices and clinics of physicians and other health practitioners is projected to increase the most rapidly throughout this period. However, not all health industries will grow at the same rapid rate. For example, hospitals, both public and

private, will continue to be the largest, but slowest growing health care industry.

Although admittedly some health care facilities do not qualify for inclusion in this book, for the sake of completeness and in order to present a more balanced picture of the health field, we have decided to exclude only health organizations operated by various government agencies.

Perhaps our best plan would be first to review the principal types of health care facilities (the workplace). Next, we shall list the principal members of the professional medical staff, the nonprofessional medical staff, and finally the support staff. Since hospitals offer the greatest variety of positions in the workplace, it seems logical to start with them.

THE WORKPLACE

Hospitals

There are approximately 6,700 hospitals in the United States. They are classified as follows:

Private institutions. These are usually owned by a group of physicians.

Nonprofit or voluntary hospitals. These are supported by patients' fees; Medicare, Medicaid, and other insurance payments; donations; and in some cases government grants for research.

Quasi-government hospitals. An example are those operated by the Veterans Administration.

Although nonprofit institutions comprise the greatest number of facilities, in reality there is no difference in the services they offer and those provided by private of government-operated hospitals. Accordingly we shall be looking at the hospital field as a whole.

"A large hospital is truly a world of its own within the outer world," said Bryan Mahan, the jovial administrator of a large eastern teaching hospital. "In our case, it's a combination of a major medical center, a college, a research center, a health care facility, a surgical facility, a hotel and restaurant business, a nursing home, and a mini-mall."

He was referring to the section of the ten-story building where, in addition to three fast-food restaurants and the hospital-operated cafeteria, there were shops operated for the convenience of patients, visitors, and hospital staff. These included a florist shop, a bookstore, a gift shop, a clothing store, a drugstore, and even a branch bank.

We were meeting in the administrator's large mahogany-paneled office furnished with a leather couch, matching chairs, and a long coffee table piled high with books and magazines. Bryan Mahan's graying hair suggested he was in his fifties, although his youthful face would lead one to think the contrary. His enthusiasm for hospital work was contagious, and we appreciated having this chance to learn the extent to which a hospital needs and can use such a wide range of job skills.

"What are the principal departments in a hospital?" we asked. "Perhaps that will give readers the best idea of how those with no medical training might fit their skills and interests into the average hospital's personnel requirements."

"I doubt any two hospitals are organized exactly alike," he replied, "so let's base our conversation on this institution, which surely is typical of most."

The administrative offices, he explained, were not unlike those of any large business. Clerks in an admitting office record pertinent background data about each new patient and then prepare all necessary paperwork including room assignment and Medicare or Medicaid insurance information. When patients check out, a cashier prepares the bill and receives payment. The accounting department has a number of bookkeepers and computer operators in addition to employees who handle payroll, pay hospital bills, collect insurance payments due, and prepare financial statements.

With some two thousand employees, the personnel purchasing department is also a busy place to work. In the personnel section employees handle details that involve interviewing and hiring applicants, putting them on the payroll, setting up personnel files, keeping track of each employee's sick and vacation days as well as salary history, and administering the employee benefits program. In the purchasing section three buyers spend all their time selecting and ordering items that range from paper clips, plasma bottles, uniforms, and x-ray equipment to air conditioners, microwave ovens, sterilizers, panel trucks, snowplows, and grass seed.

"Public relations is another important department," Mr. Mahan said. "It is also responsible for the hospital's volunteer program. This refers to the men and women who volunteer their time to staff the information desk and help wherever needed throughout the hospital, and it includes the candy stripers, the young people who want to help, too."

The housekeeping department is responsible for duties that include providing clean linens and all other supplies needed for the nursing and medical staffs; cleaning the patient and public rooms, offices, and corridors; scrubbing down walls; washing windows; waxing floors—in short, keeping the hospital as immaculate as possible.

"One department whose members are seldom seen by our patients is maintenance. These are the men and women responsible for keeping the whole hospital alive and functioning. They must be ready at a moment's notice to fix an elevator stalled between floors, repair some essential life-support equipment during an operation, or work on some delicate instruments that number in the hundreds." He paused and smiled. "I shouldn't omit replacing a burned-out bulb or frayed lamp cord. Just think of the interesting job possibilities in this department! Something is always going wrong. Pipes leak, radiators refuse to heat up, toilets stop working, air-conditioning equipment blows out hot air instead of cold—the problems can be endless! And I forgot that they also paint, cut the grass, weed the flower beds, clear the walks and driveways of snow, and provide security too!"

"Does that cover all of the nonmedical departments?" we asked.

"Yes, with the exception of food service. Those people run the huge central kitchen; purchase and store all the provisions that arrive daily by truck; and serve hundreds of patients, many of whom must follow strict diets, three times a day. They also stock the numerous little so-called pantries located all over the hospital where nurses can obtain hot and cold drinks, ice cream, and other in-between-meal snacks for patients. It's a large department that needs all kinds of personnel interested in catering and food service."

Mr. Mahan explained that the medical departments fall under the general medical administration of the hospital—nursing, obstetrics, x-ray, pediatrics, and those specialties that are directed by physicians or medical supervisors. "We provide the professional staff with everything they need to do their job, but that's as far as we go."

In response to our question about equal opportunities, Mr. Mahan commented that hospitals welcome applicants from all groups and offer them good entry-level positions. "Many people tend to think of hospitals as poor pay and difficult working conditions, but generally speaking that is not at all true today. Wages and benefits have been improving despite the serious financial problems all voluntary hospitals are experiencing."

Our last request was to talk briefly with an employee who held a position for which no specific skills or training were required.

Five minutes later, we were following Mr. Mahan into the cafeteria where he introduced us to Hernando Diaz, a short stocky young man. We shook hands with Hernando, then thanked our host and sat down.

"I could do this job most anywhere—a hotel, office building, a factory, or even a bus terminal," Hernando said. He rubbed his beard thoughtfully as he spoke.

"Why did you decide to work in a hospital?" we asked.

"I quit school in my senior year, but I couldn't find a job anywhere. Nobody even wanted to talk to me. Then a friend suggested I apply here. I did, and do you know what? This was the only place where someone talked with me. The lady told me that if I went back to school and got my diploma, some day there would be an opening for me here. I did that, and here I am!"

As custodian for the seventh floor, Hernando is responsible for keeping the public rooms, toilets, patients' rooms, offices, and corridors as spotless as possible. He has a detailed program that tells him what to do each day, and he finds it most helpful. However, when a patient checks out, Hernando must break his schedule and give that room a special cleaning, following precise instructions in order to make certain it is germ-free.

"Some people say this is woman's work," he says laughing. "Sure, most of the custodians on the other floors are ladies, but what's wrong with cleaning? My boss says he plans to promote me to the maintenance department when there's an opening. For somebody with just a high school education, I can't complain, can I?"

Hernando had to return to work, whereupon we thanked him for his time and left the cafeteria. As we rode down in the elevator crowded with doctors, nurses, and other employees who were quietly talking to each other, we felt the excitement of being part of such a large, intricate, and fascinating institution whose sole purpose is to restore people to good health.

Nursing Homes

We visited the Evergreen Nursing Home outside a large city in the Southeast. The square, one-story brick structure is built around a garden area with lawns, many trees, and flowering bushes, making it a favorite place for patients to spend part of each day. We had an appointment with Felice Gormez, a short, attractive young woman, who was assigned to show us through the facility.

"Some people think this is a dreary place to work with all these old people around," Felice said as she led us through a large living room furnished with couches and many occasional chairs. A few patients had gathered in front of the television, a foursome was playing cards, and others were sitting on the couches or slumped over asleep in their wheelchairs. We commented on the fact that there were so few men.

"That's true in most of the homes," Felice said. "Remember, on the whole, women live longer than men."

She led us down a corridor and paused at the door to one of the rooms. "A few of our folks have Alzheimer's disease," she said as she motioned to the woman asleep in her chair. "Sometimes they're difficult to handle, but it's a challenge just the same. Anyway, I enjoy my work because most patients appreciate everything we do for them. It makes the time fly, and I go home feeling good about myself."

She told us that a registered nurse is always in charge of the nursing staff, which consists of LPNs (licensed practical nurses) like herself, and CNAs (certified nursing aids). "When I come to work at quarter to seven, first thing I do is help wake up patients, wash those who can't care for themselves, and make certain that everyone is in the dining room by seven-thirty. The CNAs feed patients who cannot get to the dining room, and while everyone is eating we have a meeting with the head nurse and administrator. At the same time the maids are at work making beds and cleaning the rooms and bathrooms. The men usually do the heavy cleaning—wash and wax floors, wash windows, paint, and handle the outside work on the grounds."

We came to the dining room, a large cheery room with bright curtains and many tables for four and six. Next door was an activity room where patients could do handcrafts. At one end was a library, which patients were encouraged to use.

"Every day different events are scheduled. Today there were sitting-up exercises in the morning, this afternoon we had a picnic in the garden, and tonight is bingo. The first of each month everyone receives a calendar of events, so patients will know in advance what's scheduled for each day. The administration tries to make life as happy as possible for the men and women who must spend the rest of their lives here."

"What do the CNAs and LPNs do?" we asked.

"In this home the CNAs do much of the personal patient care, which means that they may bathe them, feed them, help change clothing, if necessary assist them in getting out of or into bed and/or their wheelchairs, and take care of bed pans or accompanying a patient to the bathroom.

"As for us LPNs, we keep the patients' charts, give out medication, handle the IVs (intravenous feeding), check on any medical problems that might arise and then consult with the registered nurse or doctor, and when necessary help the CNAs if they need a hand. There's plenty to do," she assured us, "and it all depends on how you approach your job. I like people, I enjoy helping them, and I feel good about it. If you don't like people, you shouldn't be a nurse, especially in a nursing home like this!"

Our tour concluded with a quick look at the offices, the well-equipped kitchen, and the maintenance department shops, which included the heating and air-conditioning equipment. Thus the typical nursing home is a self-contained world, somewhat like a hospital, except that it does not offer any medical services beyond nursing care.

Many hospitals operate skilled nursing facilities for patients who have had operations or serious medical problems but no longer need hospital care. In reality most of these facilities offer the same kind of nursing home care as the Evergreen Nursing Home, except that they draw upon the hospital staff and do not have a separate kitchen or their own maids and cleaners.

Physician Groups

So-called "group practice" has become increasingly popular as doctors share the cost of office space, expensive testing, x-ray and other equipment, office personnel, and other overhead. Patients tend to favor these arrangements because a group enables them to obtain broad medical care under one roof, and a doctor is always available for emergency situations.

The Caldwell Medical Group, a partnership of seven doctors, is housed in a long white building in a New England resort area. The medical staff includes two general practitioners, one pediatrician, a gynecologist, an internist, a surgeon, and a neurologist. In addition there are a physical therapist, a radiologist, and two LPNs.

We talked with Greta Hirsch, a diminutive blonde who sat erect at the reception desk.

"I'm at the center of everything!" she told us. "I make all the appointments, remind patients of their appointments the day before they're due here, greet them when they arrive, and make further appointments when they leave. Another important responsibility is recording all blood shipments to laboratories and logging in their return. In between I answer the phone, place calls for the staff, and if there's time, type letters for the manager."

She explained that a medical secretary took dictation from the doctors or transcribed from dictating machines. After a doctor sees a patient, he may dictate a report while it is fresh in his memory. Also there was a general manager, an accountant who handled all the billing and other financial affairs except the Medicare and Medicaid billing, which another person did. A custodian cleaned the offices daily, performed minor repairs, and took care of the grounds.

"This is an interesting place to work," Greta said as she put down the phone. "No two days or hours are alike. You have to handle emergencies, and there is always the person who calls in with some medical problem and asks *me*—imagine that—what to suggest when her doctor is unable to answer the phone immediately!"

Another form of group practice is the HMO (Health Maintenance Organization), which offers memberships to men and women for an annual fee. This enables members to obtain most of their medical care at a facility that can afford to purchase and maintain expensive medical equipment as well as employ a wide range of medical specialists.

Most physicians and dentists who practice alone employ a receptionist-bookkeeper and a nurse or dental assistant. Dentists, on the other hand, depending on the size of the office and practice, may employ a receptionist-bookkeeper, one or two hygienists, and a dental assistant. If two dentists share offices, the staff may be proportionately larger.

Home Health Care Agencies

As previously stated, this is the fastest growing industry in our economy. The reason is that instead of placing people in expensive nursing homes, there is a movement to keep them at home and bring health care to them. This makes sense because it is far less expensive, and the best reason for it is that most seniors dread having to be placed in a nursing home when they no longer can care for themselves in their own homes. Now, with the advent of agencies that provide nurses (registered nurses and licensed practical nurses) and certified nursing aides to schedule regular visits to homes where the family caregivers need assistance, a new era in health care is being forged.

If you have not read chapter 1, in which we visit a home health agency, we urge you to do so. There should be an increasing demand for CNAs who will find work either in home health agencies or on their own in homes where their services are needed.

Retirement and Life Care Homes

More and more older men and women are locking their front doors and moving into retirement and life care homes. Retirement homes provide a comfortable atmosphere for those who can afford to live in a facility where they have their own apartment and may either prepare their own meals or eat in a dining room operated by the facility.

Life care homes, on the other hand, are retirement homes that agree to provide the residents health care for as long as they live. To carry out this promise, a life care establishment must operate a small nursing wing complete with medical equipment and staffed with sufficient doctors and nurses at all times.

Clinics

Clinics are large or small medical centers, perhaps a department of a medical school or hospital, or even an independent establishment located in a shopping area as mentioned below.

Walk-in Clinics. A new approach to health care is the "walk-in clinic," which offers immediate medical care without need for an appointment. Depending on the community's needs, one or more doctors, specialists, and nurses may staff these offices. Some hospitals offer this type of service, others provide it only on an emergency basis; many clinics are found in shopping areas convenient to population centers.

Outpatient Clinics. This is a form of walk-in clinic, which may operate in a hospital or be part of a public health service, generally in poorer sections of a city, and primarily offers medical care either free or for a small fee to residents unable to afford regular medical care. Depending on service demands, such clinics may have one or several physicians on its staff in addition to nurse, a radiologist, a laboratory technician, and other specialists.

Other Clinics. To complete our discussion of clinics, we should mention that there are a number of well-known clinics throughout the country, most of which are connected with hospitals. Perhaps the best known would include the famous Mayo Clinic in Rochester, Minnesota; the Hitchcock Clinic in Hanover, New Hampshire; the Lovelace Clinic in Albuquerque, New Mexico; and the Leahy Clinic in Boston, Massachusetts. Patients with serious medical problems are frequently referred to one of these clinics, which specialize in treating certain diseases or medical conditions.

THE PROFESSIONALS

Physicians

The more than half million physicians are probably the most important people in the health care field. There are two types of doctors: the MD, or Doctor of Medicine, and the OD, or Doctor of Osteopathic Medicine. Although both types of physicians use traditional and accepted methods of treatment, which include drugs and surgery, the ODs emphasize the body's musculoskeletal system, believing that good health depends on the proper alignment of bones, ligaments, muscles, and nerves. Only approximately 12 percent of MDs are in general and family practice; the balance specialize.

If you are thinking of becoming a doctor, you should know that public medical schools in a recent year charged an annual tuition of $13,100 while private medical schools averaged $25,600. Room, board, medical books, and other expenses were extra. (Remember that you do not have to enter medical school immediately after college. Many men and women wait for a few years before doing this.)

Required Training. Now consider the training that is required, as reported by the *Occupational Outlook Handbook:*

> All states, the District of Columbia, and U.S. territories require physicians to be licensed. Licensure requirements for both DOs and MDs include graduation from an accredited medical school (usually 4 years), completion of a licensing examination, and between 1 and 6 years of graduate medical education, that is, a residency for MDs and an internship for DOs. Although physicians licensed in one state can usually get a license to practice in another without further examination, some states limit reciprocity. Graduates of foreign medical schools can generally begin practice in the United States after completing a U.S. hospital residency training program.
>
> The minimum educational requirement for entry to a medical or osteopathic school is 3 years of college; most applicants, however, have at least a bachelor's degree and many have advanced degrees. A few medical schools offer a combined college and medical school program that last 6 years instead of the customary 8 years.
>
> Required premedical study includes undergraduate work in physics, biology, and inorganic and organic chemistry. Students should also take courses in English, other humanities, mathematics, and the social sciences.

There are 141 medical schools in the United States—126
teach allopathic medicine and award a Doctor of Medicine
(MD); 15 teach osteopathic medicine and award the Doctor
of Osteopathic Medicine (DO). Acceptance to medical
school is very competitive. Applicants must submit tran-
scripts, scores from the Medical College Admission Test
(MCAT), and letters of recommendation. An interview with
an admissions officer may also be necessary. Character,
personality, leadership qualities, and participation in extra-
curricular activities also are considered.

Earnings. According to the American Medical Association in
1989, the average income for all physicians, after expenses, was
$155,800, making this one of the best-paid occupations. Self-
employed doctors who practiced alone or were part-owners of a
practice earned an average of $175,300. However, those in gen-
eral practice/family practice earned $95,900.

The average income for some of the specialists after expenses,
was as follows: surgery, $220,500; radiology, $210,500; obstet-
rics/gynecology, $194,300; anesthesiology, $185,800; pathology,
$154,500; internal medicine, $146,500; psychiatry, $117,700;
pediatrics, $104,700.

In addition to the costly education required to become a doctor,
those physicians who start their own practice must be prepared
to make a sizable investment when they equip their offices.
However, employment of doctors through the year 2005 is expected to grow faster than the average for all occupations due to
the steep expansion of the health care industry.

Three Other Important Medical Professionals

The following professionals must have training similar to that
outlined above for physicians.

Dentists. Nine out of ten dentists are in private practice; net median income in private practice, $80,000 a year, specialty practice, $110,000 a year.

Optometrists. Provide primary vision care; growing number in group practice; average annual income, $75,000.

Podiatrists. Most in private practice; demand expected to grow faster than average through year 2005; medium net income $73,700.

SUPPORT PERSONNEL

Medical Support Personnel

The following list includes the majority of the best known health care support positions. Except for dental assistants and hygienists, homemakers, and emergency medical technicians, these support personnel will be found in hospitals and a number of them in nursing homes, physician groups, health maintenance organizations, home health care agencies, and clinics.

Practically all of the occupations are expected to grow faster than the average through the year 2005. Earnings figures are for 1991, unless otherwise noted, and may be based on sources other than the Bureau of Labor Statistics. Each listing includes a brief job description, minimum educational years or training required beyond high school, and available earnings information.

Audiologists. Work with people who have hearing problems. Five years; median annual earnings, $26,000.

Clinical laboratory technologists. Examine and analyze body fluid, cells, and tissue; interpret results; and send them to physicians. Four years; average hourly earnings, $14.71.

Dental assistants. Perform a variety of duties including working with dentists as they examine and treat patients. One year but most assistants train on the job; median weekly earnings, $300.

Dental hygienists. Examine, clean patients' teeth and mouth, help patient develop good oral health. One year; average hourly earnings, $17.50 (1989).

Dieticians. Provide nutritional services for patients in hospitals and nursing homes. Five years; median annual earnings, $27,268 (1990).

EEG technologists. Operate EEG (electroencephalograph) machines, which record brain waves. One year on the job; average hourly earnings, $10.70.

EKG technologists. Operate electrocardiograph machines, which trace impulses transmitted by the heart. Most training done on the job; average hourly earnings, $8.66. *Note:* Employment expected to decline.

Emergency medical technicians. Better known as EMTs, they give immediate care to people needing urgent medical attention, then take them to a medical facility. Requirements include 80–100 hours of classroom work, 10 hours in a hospital; average annual starting earnings, $21,650.

Homemaker-home health aides. Help aged, disabled, and housebound persons to live in their own homes instead of an institution; also help in families where there are children and one or both parents are incapacitated. In some areas aides must pass a competency test for which training may be taken; usually start as cleaners, later assuming personal duties; starting hourly earnings, $4.25, but in cities where cost of living is high, rate may reach $10.00.

Laboratory technicians. Perform routine tests and laboratory procedures. Two years; average hourly earnings, $11.33.

Licensed practical nurses (LPNs). Perform usual nursing duties under supervision of a physician or registered nurse. One year; median weekly earnings, $377 (1990).

Medical assistants. Help physician treat and examine patients and perform routine tasks in the office. On-the-job training, although programs are offered in vocational/technical schools, colleges, and universities; average starting annual earnings for graduates of accredited schools, $14,000 (1990).

Medical record technicians. Organize and evaluate patients' medical files. Two years; average hourly earnings, $9.70.

Nursing aids (called certified nursing aides, CNAs, in some localities). May be principal caregiver in nursing homes; in hospitals, answer patients' call bells, serve meals, make beds, feed, dress, and bathe patients, and may do many other tasks. Neither high school diploma nor experience necessary in some cases, but many employers require new workers to complete seventy-five hours of training and pass a test within four months of employment; median annual earnings, $13,000 (1990).

Pharmacists. Dispense medicines, drugs, and other items prescribed by doctors, dentists, and podiatrists. Five years in accredited College of Pharmacy; median annual income, $41,300 (1990).

Physicians assistants. Trained to perform many of the time-consuming but routine tasks physicians normally do. Two years; median annual salary, $33,971 (1990).

Psychiatric aides. Care for emotionally disturbed or mentally impaired patients. Neither high school diploma nor experience may be required, but some states require formal training program; median annual earnings, $13,100 (1990).

Radiologic (x-ray) technologists. Take and process x-ray pictures of the human body for use in diagnosing medical problems; may also operate more advanced mechanical equipment such as the magnetic resonance imaging (MRI) machine or equipment coupled to computers to enhance their x-ray capability. One to four years; average hourly earnings, $12.75.

Registered nurses (RNs). As private care nurses, care for patients who need skilled nursing care in their own homes; as nursing home nurses, manage nursing care for residents; as hospital nurses (the largest group), supervise licensed practical nurses and aides, carry out medical orders of physicians, and give bedside care; as office nurses, assist physicians who are in private practice. Four years; must graduate from an accredited nursing school and pass a national licensing examination; average hourly earnings in hospitals, $16.20, nursing homes, $12.96, but nurse specialists earn more.

Respiratory therapists. Evaluate, treat, and care for patients with breathing problems. Two years; average hourly earnings, $12.60.

Surgical technologists. Assist doctors, surgeons, and others in operating room. One to two years; average hourly earnings, $10.03.

Therapists, occupational. Help patients who have disabling physical conditions develop, maintain, or recover daily living and work skills. Four years; median annual earnings, $30,500 (1990).

Therapists, physical. Help patients relieve pain and improve mobility and limit permanent disabilities of patients who have disease or injuries. Four years; average hourly earnings, $17.01.

Therapists, recreational. Use approved activities to maintain or treat emotional, mental, or physical well-being of patients. Four years; average annual earnings in nursing homes between $15,000 and $20,000.

Nonmedical Support Personnel

As has been shown throughout this chapter, there are numerous nonmedical support occupations in the health care industry. We list below some of the principal job titles, most of which have been mentioned. All of these can be entry-level positions. Most require a high school diploma and one or two years' training in a vocational/technical school, community college, or other institution of higher education. See the Suggested Readings in appendix A for books that will give you further information about them.

Accounting clerk	Library assistant
Air-conditioning technician	Maid
Ambulance driver/attendant	Mail clerk
Baker	Order clerk
Billing clerk	Painter
Carpenter	Payroll/timekeeping clerk
Cleaner/custodian	Personnel clerk
Computer operator	Receptionist
Computer programmer	Refrigeration technician
Cook	Secretary
Data entry keyer	Security guard
Electrician	Statistical clerk
Elevator mechanic	Stenographer
File clerk	Telephone operator
Groundsperson	Typist
Heating technician	Word processor
Laundry machine operator	

MEDICAL RESEARCH

One aspect of the health care industry is medical research, which is conducted by the federal government, universities, medical centers, and pharmaceutical manufacturers. If research is your ultimate goal, it would be wise to find out what educational preparation you will need for the field in which you hope to work. You should plan on at least four years of college and depending on your goal, one to three additional years of study. Of course, there are support positions that do not require such extensive training.

Our advice for those interested in this overall subject is to discuss your plans with your guidance counselor and/or write to the National Institutes of Health, the government agency that conducts and supports biomedical research, research training, and the development of research resources. For further information, write to the Public Information Office, National Institutes of Health, Bethesda, MD 20892.

HEALTH CARE ORGANIZATIONS

You may want to find a career somewhere within the health industry but not in a hospital, doctor's or dentist's office, home health agency, or other organization concerned with delivering direct health care. If so, you might consider finding a position with one of the many national health care organizations, which employ a wide range of office personnel and offer interesting career possibilities. There are hundreds of agencies specializing in a broad spectrum of health problems. Many are very small, a few employ hundreds of men and women, and those listed below are believed to employ a minimum of ten on their staffs. We have endeavored to include those agencies that deal with major diseases or health problems.

In addition the following list will provide a source for further information about the types of jobs discussed in this chapter.

Alzheimer's Association
    70 East Lake Street
    Chicago, IL 60601

American Academy of Allergy and Immunology
    611 East Wells Street
    Milwaukee, WI 53202

American Academy of Pediatrics
P. O. Box 927
Elk Grove Village, IL 60009

American Academy of Physicians Assistants
950 North Washington Street
Alexandria, VA 22314

American Association of Colleges of Pharmacy
1426 Prince Street
Alexandria, VA 22314

American Association of Medical Assistants
20 North Wacker Drive
Chicago, IL 60606

American Board of Registration for Electroencephalographic
Technologists
P. O. Box 11434
Norfolk, VA 23517

American Cancer Society
1599 Clifton Road NE
Atlanta, GA 30329

American Chiropractic Association
1701 Clarendon Boulevard
Arlington, VA 22209

American Dental Assistants Association
919 North Michigan Avenue
Chicago, IL 60611

American Dental Association
211 East Chicago Avenue
Chicago, IL 60611

American Dental Hygienists Association
211 East Chicago Avenue
Chicago, IL 60611

American Diabetes Association
1660 Duke Street
Alexandria, VA 22314

American Dietetic Association
216 West Jackson Boulevard
Chicago, IL 60606

American Geriatrics Society
770 Lexington Avenue
New York, NY 10021

American Health Care Association
1201 L Street NW
Washington, DC 20005

American Heart Association
7320 Greenville Avenue
Dallas, TX 75231

American Hospital Association
840 North Lake Shore Drive
Chicago, IL 60611

American Hospital Association
Division of Nursing
840 North Lake Shore Drive
Chicago, IL 60611

American Kidney Fund
6110 Executive Boulevard
Rockville, MD 20552

American Lung Association
1740 Broadway
New York, NY 10019

American Medical Association
515 North State Street
Chicago, IL 60610

American Medical Records Association
919 North Michigan Avenue
Chicago, IL 60611

American Medical Technologists
710 Higgins Road
Park Ridge, IL 60068

American Medical Women Association
   801 North Fairfax Street
   Alexandria, VA 22314

American Nurses Association
   2420 Pershing Road
   Kansas City, MO 64108

American Occupational Therapy Association
   1383 Piccard Drive
   Rockville, MD 20850

American Osteopathic Association
   142 East Orleans Street
   Chicago, IL 60611

American Physical Therapy Association
   1111 North Fairfax Street
   Alexandria, VA 22314

American Society of Hospital Pharmacists
   4630 Montgomery Avenue
   Bethesda, MD 20814

American Society of Radiologic Technologists
   15000 Central Avenue SE
   Albuquerque, NM 87123

Association of Surgical Technologists
   7108-C South Alton Way
   Englewood, CO 80112

Building Service Contractors Association International
   10201 Lee Highway
   Fairfax, VA 22030

Cystic Fibrosis Foundation
   6931 Arlington Road
   Bethesda, MD 20814

Educational Foundation of the National Restaurant Association
   250 South Wacker Drive
   Chicago, IL 60606

Foundation for the Blind
  15 West Sixteenth Street
  New York, NY 10011

Foundation for Hospice and Home Care/National Home Caring
  Council
  519 C Street NE
  Washington, DC 20002

National AIDS Network
  2033 M Street NW
  Washington, DC 20036

National Association for the Deaf
  814 Thayer Avenue
  Silver Spring, MD 20910

National Association of Emergency Medical Technicians
  9140 Ward Parkway
  Kansas City, MO 64114

National Association for Home Care
  519 C Street NE
  Washington, DC 20002

The National Board for Respiratory Care, Inc.
  8310 Nieman Road
  Lenexa, KS 66214

National Federation of Licensed Practical Nurses, Inc.
  P. O. Box 1088
  Raleigh, NC 27619

National Health Council
  350 Fifth Avenue
  New York, NY 10018

National Institute of Electromedical Information
  P. O. Box 4633
  Bay Terrace, NY 11360

National League for Nursing
  350 Hudson Street
  New York, NY 10014

National Mental Health Association
  1021 Prince Street
  Alexandria, VA 22314

National Multiple Sclerosis Society
  205 East Forty-second Street
  New York, NY 10017

National Parkinson's Disease Foundation
  1501 NW Ninth Avenue
  Miami, FL 33136

National Society of Cardiovascular Technology
  1101 Fourteenth Street NW
  Washington, DC 20005

Society of Nuclear Medicine
  136 Madison Avenue
  New York, NY 10016

CHAPTER 6

CAREERS IN SOCIAL SCIENCE

Inspire me with love for my art and for Your creatures.
Do not allow thirst for profit, ambition for renown and
admiration to interfere with my profession. For these are
the enemies of truth and can lead me astray in the great task
of attending to the welfare of Your creatures. Preserve the
strength of my body and soul that they may be ever ready
to help rich and poor, good and bad, enemy as well as
friend. In the sufferer let me see only the human being.
                                —Prayer of Maimonides
                    12th century physician and philosopher

You will find as many definitions of the term *social work* as
there are workers in the field. Social work means helping people
in need. Such men and women may require money, medical
attention, psychiatric assistance, vocational guidance, family
counseling, or other special services that will help them conquer
their troubles. The aid is brought by social workers, men and
women who are professionally trained and often highly skilled in
their field. They assist those who have problems and endeavor to
enable them to realize happy and satisfying lives. Social work
can bring great personal rewards to those who pursue the profession.

Throughout the nineteenth century the approach to helping the
poor, sick, and handicapped remained one of making it as un-

pleasant as possible in order to discourage people from seeking such aid. Many still believed that the poor and sick were unfit, unworthy members of society. However, by the time America entered World War I in 1917, a new attitude toward welfare had emerged.

Instead of considering poverty and physical and mental handicaps as personal disgraces for which nothing could be done, forward-looking individuals began to urge that people so affected be treated like human beings who could be rehabilitated to become useful and self-supporting citizens. Still, by 1930, little had been done for these unfortunate persons. In New York City the needy and indigent were dependent on such charity as the private social-service agencies could dispense. Once the staggering burden of feeding and caring for unemployed was added to their other responsibilities, their funds proved insufficient, and they could not help all the deserving poor who came for food, clothing, and shelter, to say nothing of other assistance. The Depression was to change this method of caring for the needy after the New Deal was established. Hereafter the federal government would have to step in and provide massive and continuous grants from its vast financial resources to feed the hungry and provide unemployment relief.

Poverty is not the sole problem that plagues America, however. In too many families the children know only the misery of a broken home as parents seek divorce and fathers disappear. Crimes of all kinds are increasing at an alarming rate, accompanied by a frightening rise in cases of drug addiction and alcoholism. The number of Americans who are mentally disturbed severely taxes the capacities of hospitals and clinics. Millions of aged have scarcely enough income to keep them alive. Substandard housing exists in country and town alike, but the slums and ghettos found in the metropolitan areas call for immediate attention. All these problems fall into the laps of the social workers.

THE SOCIAL WORKER

"I'm a failure," the middle-aged man said as he looked away from the social worker who sat across from him in an office of a family agency. "I don't know why I came," Mr. Benton continued. "There's nothing you can do for me."

Mr. Benton had lost his job as a meat cutter when the packing plant where he worked closed, and that very same day the doctor told his wife that she required a serious and expensive operation. Little wonder he was upset and discouraged.

"I'm sure we can help you." The social worker's voice was so calm and reassuring that Mr. Benton turned toward her. For the first time in days his face broke into a faint smile. It took several days, but the social worker assisted Mr. Benton in taking an inventory of his job skills. With new confidence he went out and found a position where his experience and abilities were needed. Meanwhile the social worker arranged to finance Mrs. Benton's operation.

The above case is typical of how a social worker helps people individually and in family units. Casework is the very core of social work—although by no means all of it. The principal method by which social agencies help is through social casework. This is the only way the representative of an agency can become acquainted with the problems of the individual or family unit and learn all the necessary facts that will enable him or her to recommend or take corrective action. Assigning a caseworker to a problem is expensive, but it is the surest way the job can be done thoroughly.

The so-called family social agency is one of the oldest types of social service organizations, because the first efforts to help were focused on poor families. Today these agencies offer a variety of special services to clients who come voluntarily when they need assistance. Once a client has contacted a social service agency and indicated a need for help, he or she is invited to come to the office for an initial discussion. Years ago the caseworker would have visited the client in his or her residence, but today such visits are usually undertaken only if the caseworker needs to observe the client in the home environment and learn how the various members of the family interact.

The initial interview, called the "intake interview," is often difficult for the client, who may be embarrassed at having to discuss personal problems. At this time the caseworker must decide whether the person can be helped, if the problem is as serious as represented, if the client has the ability to change, and whether the agency has the resources to help the client. Fees are discussed because the agency expects the client to pay at least in proportion to his or her financial ability.

The nature of the client's problem will determine whom he or she will see in the agency. In some small agencies each staff member can handle all problems that are accepted. In others there may be specialists on the staff, such as marriage counselors, psychiatrists, vocational guidance counselors, and lawyers. If after several interviews, it is determined that the client's problem cannot be solved, the social worker plans to terminate the relationship and may refer the client to another agency. On the other hand, cases that have been successfully closed are often given a routine follow-up visit in six months or a year to check on the client's progress and determine whether the problem has been permanently solved.

PERSONAL APTITUDES

It is not enough to like, understand, and want to help people to be successful in social work. Other personal traits and aptitudes are necessary, too. The principal ones include:

- Ability to read with comprehension and express yourself clearly in writing and speech
- Desire to apply ideas and imagination to your work each day
- Perseverance that will ensure your completing whatever you undertake, no matter how difficult the task
- Ability to take directions and work with others as a member of a team
- Curiosity that will make you want to discover the causes of the human or social problems or difficulties you encounter
- Cheerfulness that is strong enough to carry you through unhappy or unpleasant work experiences
- Interest in reading and learning, because social workers are forever seeking new knowledge and better ways of doing their job
- Tolerance that will enable you to work with people whose standards of cleanliness and morality may be unlike your own
- Insight that will enable you to determine your inner strengths and weaknesses plus will power that is strong enough to make you correct your deficiencies

THE WORKING AREAS

Work with Individuals

- Helping individuals, families, and the aged with every kind of personal problem and securing financial aid as well as the necessary health and other services that they need
- Counseling the handicapped, such as the blind, crippled, or disabled

- Placing children in foster homes or arranging for their adoption
- Working in medical or psychiatric clinics and hospitals as a member of a rehabilitation team

Agencies and institutions that offer career opportunities include child care and adoption agencies, child guidance clinics, churches, correctional and protective institutions, family service agencies, hospitals, military establishments, programs for the aged, public welfare and health departments, rehabilitation centers, schools and day nurseries, and services for displaced persons and travelers.

Work with Communities

- Helping the community plan for and operate necessary welfare services
- Coordinating existing community social services
- Encouraging and helping citizens to become leaders in the social welfare field
- Raising funds and budgeting the monies needed for health and welfare agencies

Agencies and institutions that offer career opportunities include community welfare councils, housing bureaus, intergroup relations organizations, neighborhood centers, social action and planning bodies, and united funds.

Work in Social Research

- Obtaining, studying, and interpreting special data and information to determine (1) the various social services needed in a community and to what extent they are being provided; (2) the needs of particular services and groups; and (3) better

methods of conducting casework and providing other services
- Devising methods of measuring the cost of social services and their effectiveness

Agencies and institutions that offer career opportunities include national social service agencies such as Family Service Association of America and United Community Funds and Councils of America; schools of social work; government agencies such as the Bureau of Family Services or the Children's Bureau; and a few of the larger local agencies such as the Community Service Society of New York.

Work in Social Administration

- Planning and directing the overall program of a social service or public welfare agency
- Employing, training, and supervising staff members
- Providing leadership in drawing up policies and operating procedures
- Administering financial affairs
- Cooperating with other public and private health and welfare agencies

Agencies and institutions that offer career opportunities include all public and private social service and health agencies.

Work in Teaching

- Teaching in graduate schools of social service
- Giving field instruction in social agencies

Agencies and institutions that offer career opportunities include colleges, graduate schools of social work, medical schools, social agencies, and theological seminaries.

THE TYPICAL JOBS

For all of the jobs listed here, except the two preceded by an asterisk, you will need special training in social work.

Administrator. The man or woman who holds this title is the top executive of any social service or public welfare agency or institution. He or she is responsible for all planning, handling of finances, and directing of the entire operation (generally with the aid of a staff).

Administrative assistant. Acts as an assistant to an administrator or other top executive. Performs various assignments and, in the superior's absence, may assume his or her duties and responsibilities.

Case consultant. An experienced caseworker or social worker who counsels other social workers as well as those laypeople and professionals who are involved in some aspect of social work but have no training in the field.

Caseworker. A trained social service worker who investigates cases of personal and family maladjustment and need and who gives advice and assistance.

Community organization worker. A social worker who specializes in helping the various agencies in a community work together more effectively.

Department head. The executive who directs all of the activities of a single department within an organization and who is responsible for everything that is done within the unit.

Director of fund-raising. An executive who organizes and supervises all aspects of a campaign to solicit funds for a church, volunteer health or welfare agency, or other philanthropic institutions. Should have at least a college degree with emphasis on courses in social service.

Director of public relations. A person trained in the art of public relations who is in charge of a public relations department or responsible for the public relations function of an organization. Training should be obtained in a university that has a school of public relations.

Field supervisor. A staff member of a social service agency or a university professor to whom a student reports while he or she is obtaining training in the field (i.e., a social service agency) as part of a postgraduate study in social work.

Group worker. A social worker who specializes in working with groups of people rather than individuals.

Research director. A social worker who plans and administers all of the work of a research staff, which collects, analyzes, and interprets data for a government or voluntary social work agency.

Teacher. A trained social worker who joins the faculty of a school that offers courses in social work or awards graduate degrees in the field.

THE BENEFITS

Good opportunities for promotion exist in the social work field because of the shortage of qualified personnel. You will find it possible to move from one kind of practice to another without being forced to become a specialist who is then frozen into one kind of job. Women who marry and leave work to raise a family may expect a warm welcome if they wish to return in later years.

Working conditions are good in the social work field. In most agencies you can expect:

- Liberal annual paid vacations
- Generous sick leave
- Health and hospitalization insurance

- Retirement plans (in addition to Social Security coverage)
- Good personnel practices in handling employees

You will receive all these benefits in most vocations, but social work offers a big added plus—the satisfaction of helping people. No matter what your job in social work, whether it is typing reports or counseling a distraught mother, you are part of a team effort the goal of which is to aid those in need or in trouble.

These are some of the satisfactions this added plus should give you:

- The inner happiness that comes from being of help to your less fortunate neighbors
- The joy that helping brings, especially when the help enables a person to recognize personal problems and draw on his or her own resources and courage to solve them
- The fun of using your imagination and initiative on the job
- The excitement that comes from achieving improvements in a community's social situation
- The challenge of working with people, identifying their real problems, and finding solutions for them

EARNINGS

Social workers held about 438,000 jobs in 1990, with two out of five positions being in state, county, or municipal government agencies. A bachelor's degree is the minimum requirement for most positions, with a master's degree in social work needed for a majority of the health and mental health jobs. Average annual earnings for the overall types of settings averaged between $23,000 and $36,000 annually.

Human services workers (social service technician, case management aide, social work assistant, residential counselor, alcohol or drug abuse counselor, child abuse worker, community outreach worker, mental health technician, or gerontology aide, for example) had annual starting salaries ranging from $12,000 to $20,000, with experienced workers making from $15,000 to $25,000 annually.

More than half of the 194,000 recreational workers were employed by park and recreational departments of county and municipal agencies, about 15 percent in nonprofit organizations (civic, social, fraternal, religious), and about 12 percent were in programs run by social service organizations (halfway houses, group homes, institutions for delinquent youths). The median annual earnings were about $16,000, but managerial and supervisory positions ranged from $22,000 to $95,000 annually, depending on the level of responsibility and size of staff.

Most of the above positions are expected to grow faster than the average for all occupations through the year 2005.

FOR FURTHER INFORMATION

Information about social service can be as close as your telephone or available from one of more than 1,700 national social service agencies in the United States. A typical listing in the yellow pages of the phone book, under "Social and Human Services," lists these categories of local agencies: blind organizations and services; family and individual services; foster care services; health services; housing assistance; human services; and mental health services.

Some of the larger national agencies that are sources of further information as well as job possibilities appear below, but you are advised to consult the Gale *Encyclopedia of Associations* for a more complete listing.

Al-Anon Family Group Headquarters
    P. O. Box 862
    Midtown Station
    New York, NY 10018

American Association for Counseling and Development
    5999 Stevenson Avenue
    Alexandria, VA 22304

American Association of Retired Persons
    601 E Street NW
    Washington, DC 20049

American Correctional Association
    8025 Laurel Lakes Court
    Laurel, MD 20707

American Red Cross
    431 Eighteenth Street NW
    Washington, DC 20006

American Society on Aging
    833 Market Street
    San Francisco, CA 94103

Child Welfare League of America
    440 First Street NW
    Washington, DC 20001

Children's Defense Fund
    122 C Street NW
    Washington, DC 20001

Family Service of America
    11700 West Lake Park Drive
    Milwaukee, WI 53224

"Just Say No" International
    2101 Webster Street
    Oakland Creek, CA 94612

Kiwanis International
    3636 Woodview Terrace
    Indianapolis, IN 46268

National Adoption Center
　1218 Chestnut STreet
　Philadelphia, PA 19107

National Association for Retarded Citizens
　500 East Border Street
　Arlington, TX 76010

National Association of Social Workers
　7981 Eastern Avenue
　Silver Spring, MD 20910

National Council of Senior Citizens
　1331 F Street NW
　Washington, DC 20004

National Council on the Aging
　409 Third Street NW
　Washington, DC 20024

National Council on Alcoholism
　12 West Twenty-first Street
　New York, NY 10010

National Council on Crime and Delinquency
　685 Market Street
　San Francisco, CA 94105

National Recreation and Park Association
　3101 Park Center Drive
　Alexandria, VA 22303

National Right to Life Committee
　419 Seventh Street
　Washington, DC 20004

National Safe Kids Campaign
　111 Michigan Avenue NW
　Washington, DC 20010

National Safety Council
　425 North Michigan Avenue
　Chicago, IL 60611

National Volunteer Center
    736 Jackson Place NW
    Washington, DC 20006

Planned Parenthood
    810 Seventh Avenue
    New York, NY 10018

Rotary International
    1560 Sherman Avenue
    Evanston, IL 60201

Save the Children Federation
    54 Wilton Road
    Westport, CT 06880

CHAPTER 7

EDUCATION

Please don't skip this chapter because you have no interest in becoming a teacher! Every school, college, and university also must have a nonteaching support staff. A small school may have a few employees, whereas in a large college* there might be over a thousand men and women who are not faculty members. As you will see, educational institutions require a broad range of employees who have diverse skills and responsibilities. You might well fill one of these positions.

Because this book is concerned only with nonprofit organizations, all government jobs are excluded. Public elementary and high schools are tax supported as are state colleges and their branches, most community colleges, and many vocational/technical schools. Although these comprise the bulk of our vast educational system, there are many private schools and colleges and it is with them that we are concerned. However, it should be pointed out that most of the career possibilities touched on here are also available in parts of the public education sector.

---

*To make for easier reading throughout this chapter, we will use the word "college" to mean a college and/or university.

PROFESSIONAL SUPPORT STAFF POSITIONS

There are a number of nonteaching positions in schools and colleges that call for college-trained professionals. The principal ones are:

Librarians

Depending on the size of the library, there may be openings for men and women who have received their master's degree in library service. Some librarians hire employees who are studying for their library degree or have taken some courses in librarianship. (See chapter 4.)

Financial Personnel

With annual tuition rates in some colleges soaring over $20,000, education has become big business. Schools and colleges must be run in a businesslike manner. This calls for employees whose titles may range from bursar (who may handle all the financial affairs of a small school) to the financial vice president of a college to whom a large staff may report. College-trained accountants and other financial specialists find positions in many schools and colleges.

Director of Development

This branch is responsible for raising money since practically every educational institution that is not tax supported must obtain financial help to close the gap between the fees students pay and the actual operating costs. (Some tax-supported colleges also have development departments to raise money. See chapter 11.)

Director of Public Relations

See chapter 1 for a discussion of public relations.

Admissions Director

This function is becoming increasingly important because of the large number of students seeking admission to private schools and institutions of higher education. Although most schools prefer to hire college graduates as admissions directors, in one private school a secretary who had unusual rapport with the students as well as administrative abilities was appointed admissions director, even though she lacked a college degree. A faculty committee had responsibility for passing on all her recommendations. Smaller colleges may hire an alumnus for the post, but large colleges usually seek men and women who have had previous experience in other institutions. A good way to enter this field is to obtain a job as recruiter or interviewer in an admissions department.

Computer Specialists

Today most schools and colleges have fairly sophisticated computer systems. Not only are many of an institution's records available on computer disks, but the library probably has its own extensive computer operations. Various computer specialists are needed to service and install computer equipment as well as enter data on the computer disks.

Personnel Director

Where large numbers of employees work for a school or college, the personnel director is an important member of the nonteaching staff. The usual responsibilities of this department include employee indoctrination and training programs, administration of the benefits program (pension, insurance, paid holidays, sick leave), keeping personnel records, and hiring and firing. The director is usually college-trained and may have done graduate work in personnel administration. Depending on the nature of the position on the personnel staff, a college degree may be required.

Purchasing Director

The purchasing director of a large college is responsible for buying everything from pencils, blackboard erasers, microscopes, mops, food, and washing machines to grass seed, lawn mowers, football uniforms, and patrol cars for the campus police. This position calls for someone who knows where to find sources of supply, how to deal with vendors to get the best buy for the least money, and how to purchase in order to protect the college against fraud and shoddy goods. Men and women called "buyers" are the chief purchasing department members, each of whom is responsible for a different area of purchasing and thus a specialist in that field. The director supervises all of the buyers and may handle some of the most difficult purchases personally. He or she also is available to consult with faculty members and other employees regarding their needs. Most purchasing directors are expected to have a college degree and preferably a master's in business administration.

Athletic Coach

Sports being an important part of most school and college programs, the position of coach or trainer is held in high regard in most places. A degree in physical education plus an outstanding record in one or two sports are the usual requirements for this post.

Although salary and wage scales of these nonprofit institutions may be lower than those of tax-supported schools and colleges, as well as business and industry, most educational employers offer good job security and many have employee benefits programs. For the most part schools and colleges are more relaxed workplaces than you will find in business and industry, an advantage that may appeal to you.

To learn about possible job openings at a school, go directly to the administration building where someone will direct you to the personnel department.

For further information contact one or more of the following organizations, some of which may offer interesting career possibilities:

American Association of Collegiate Registrars and Admissions
    Officers
1 Dupont Circle
Washington, DC 20036

American Association of School Personnel Administrators
825 Lurline Drive
Foster City, CA 94404

College and University Personnel Association
1233 Twentieth Street NW
Washington, DC 20036

International Association of Campus Law Enforcement Administrators
638 Prospect Avenue
Hartford, CT 06105

National Association of College Admissions Counselors
1800 Diagonal Road
Alexandria, VA 22314

National Association of Educational Buyers
180 Froehlich Farm Boulevard
Woodbury, NY 11797

National Association of Purchasing Management
  P. O. Box 22160
  Tempe, AZ 85282

National Association of School Security Directors
  P. O. Box 31338
  Temple Hills, MD 20748

National Collegiate Athletic Association
  P. O. Box 1906
  Mission, KS 66201

National High School Athletic Coaches Association
  P. O. Box 1808
  Ocala, FL 32678

Special Interest Group for University and College Computing Services
  P. O. Box 3842
  Seal Beach, CA 90740

NONPROFESSIONAL SUPPORT STAFF

There is a fairly wide range of job opportunities for those who do not have a college degree but have learned a skill at a postgraduate vocational/technical school or junior college. There are also openings for unskilled workers who receive on-the-job training. Perhaps one of the following positions will interest you.

Office Personnel

Clerical and secretarial workers will find their services needed in every school and college. The larger the institution, the more plentiful the positions and variety of responsibilities.

Maintenance Personnel

Men and women who are responsible for painting, plumbing, carpentry, electrical work, repairs, and maintaining the heating, air-conditioning, electrical, and other mechanical equipment are always in demand.

Custodians

These employees are responsible for housekeeping duties such as cleaning classrooms and lecture rooms, restrooms, storerooms, corridors, stairways, dining halls, dormitories, kitchens, and public areas.

Groundskeepers

If you like outdoor work, you may find openings for a position tending the lawns and shrubbery, trees and flower beds, as well as clearing sidewalks and roads of ice and snow during the winter. Sometimes these employees also do painting and other maintenance chores.

Security Guards

Many campuses have their own security or police force to patrol the grounds and buildings, direct traffic, and provide protection for all within the college campus community.

TEACHING IN PRIVATE SCHOOLS

We telephoned Delores Diaz who teaches at an "exclusive" girls' school in a large West Coast city. "Could you please tell us something about your job?" we asked.

"Certainly," she responded. "To begin, let me say that I teach dance and physical education. Classes are held from nine until three with a half-hour lunch period. I have a gym class every period, and after school I teach dance to those students who elect it as an activity." She paused for a moment, then continued.

"I surely have it a lot easier than those who teach academic subjects, because they have to prepare lesson plans, correct homework, and also prepare and correct exam papers. Of course, I have to grade all my students on their phys ed classwork, but that's a lot easier and less time-consuming for me than for an English or Latin teacher, for example."

"Do you feel it's a disadvantage for a private school to be located in the center of a large city?"

"No!" she replied emphatically. "In fact, it's a great advantage, because the school administration encourages us to seek out the rich cultural activities and performing arts that surround us. This is certainly an added dimension to our educational program and is great for those of us who live nearby."

"Where do you live?"

"My apartment's but a short bus ride from the school, and I can walk in good weather. It's an ideal life for one who loves the city and all it has to offer. With a ten-week vacation, I have ample time for travel. But," she added, "it's definitely not for the individual who does not enjoy big-city living. I'd advise such a teacher to seek a job elsewhere."

We asked if she cared to make any other observations.

"Yes, I should point out that most private schools are struggling financially, and many cannot afford to pay salaries such as you will find in nearby public schools. At times we have to tighten our belts, so to speak, and expected or well-deserved raises are not always forthcoming. Living in any metropolitan area is expensive, which means a teacher has to stretch his or her salary to meet expenses. But this is offset if one truly enjoys one's surroundings and feels that his or her efforts are appreciated by both students and the school administration."

In contrast to Delores, Clifton Harmes teaches French, Spanish, and Latin in a typical "country day school" in Connecticut.

"I enjoy the luxury of teaching small classes," he told us. "You have no discipline problems, you get to know your students, and you can help them with their weak areas. Our school has excellent athletic fields and other sports facilities, and I like coaching soccer and tennis in season. There's a strong school spirit here; many students come from affluent homes and are expected to go on to college.

"That," he quickly added, "is one disadvantage of teaching in this kind of school. Although parents expect their children to enter the top colleges and universities, the students don't always adopt the same goals! Hence there's sometimes friction between parents who are paying enormous tuition bills and faculty who are doing their best to prepare their pupils to score successfully on the endless college entrance examinations. However, I guess this is a problem in many private schools."

Another cause for complaint is the fact that Clifton commutes from nearby New York State, where he lives with a friend who teaches in a public school located in a well-to-do town. The friend makes almost twice Clifton's salary, and Clifton would like to find a comparable position in a public school.

"It's tough to live on my salary," Clifton confided in us, "however, my friend has pointed out that I'd be exchanging the country-club atmosphere of the private school for the disadvantages of the public school system with its much larger classes, disruptive and often violent students, as well as bureaucratic administration. Still," he added, "I'd like that larger income and what it would buy!"

As this book goes to press, Clifton is completing courses necessary to obtain certification in New York State and thus enable him to apply for a teaching position. He is an example of how a new teacher can find an opening in a private school, obtain experience, and later transfer to a better-paying public school system. However, not every teacher in a private school has this goal, as we shall see in the case of Paul Bent.

Perhaps Paul Bent, the headmaster of a small private boarding school in a small Illinois town, has the best of all worlds. He lives in a comfortable house on campus provided by the school. He and his family enjoy his generous vacations in northern Minnesota, although like many private school headmasters and faculty members, he must watch his expenses.

"It was not always like this," Paul told us. "When I first joined the faculty, my wife and I were responsible for one of the dormitories. We had a small apartment and there seemed scarcely a night we did not have to discipline some student for infraction of rules. Also we had to eat all our meals in the student dining room—sitting at the head of a table for ten and trying to maintain a semblance of decorum. That was not fun during the first years, but there were good times too; and now that we have a family and I have the top administrative job, we live apart from the school and only have to go up to the dining room on special occasions.

"I think there are tradeoffs in every job," he continued. "I enjoyed teaching small classes and never considered transferring to a better paying job in a public school system. I like the communal life of a so-called boarding school. Best of all my family and I have our own home, which is something we might not be able to afford otherwise. You become attached to a school like this, and it provides a sense of security and satisfaction in being part of an institution that is preparing young people for college or further training that will enable them to launch their own careers."

A college degree is a must for teaching in any private elementary or secondary school. Some schools have other requirements, which you can learn only by applying for a position. To obtain information about specific private schools, consult *The Handbook of Private Schools: An Annual Descriptive Survey of Inde-*

pendent Education, published by Porter Sargent Publishers (Boston), which you may find in your local public library.

According to the National Education Association, public elementary school teachers averaged about $32,400 a year in 1991 and secondary school teachers $33,700. Teachers' earnings in private schools were lower for the most part.

TEACHING IN COLLEGES AND UNIVERSITIES

College and university faculties held 712,000 jobs in 1990, most of them being in public institutions. Although this book is concerned only with nonprofit organizations, most state universities are considered nonprofit schools because they depend greatly on philanthropy to help them meet their expenses. Thus if you are interested in a teaching career in the field of higher education, we suggest you apply wherever you feel the opportunities would be greatest for you. Although the ten so-called "Ivy League" colleges and "Seven Sisters" are private colleges, many state universities are equally prestigious, and there are also small colleges well worth investigating.

There are four academic ranks within which members of college and university faculty fall: professors, associate professors, assistant professors, and instructors. A few members are lecturers. New faculty members are usually hired as instructors or assistant professors. However, if you have a master's degree or Ph.D., you will probably qualify for a better starting position.

The employment outlook for college and university faculty is expected to increase as fast as the average of all occupations through the year 2005 as enrollments increase and many faculty members retire. The average salary for full professors was $56,200, associate professors $41,800, assistant professors $34,600, and instructors $26,100. According to a 1990–91 survey by the American Association of University Professors, full-time faculty members with nine-month contracts averaged $43,700. Those who taught on eleven- or twelve-month contracts earned more. Remember, however, that these are average figures and beginning salaries would be less.

For more information about teaching careers, consult the Suggested Readings in appendix A at the end of this book, or write one or more of the following organizations:

Academic Alliances
   c/o American Association for Higher Education
   One Dupont Circle
   Washington, DC 20036

American Association of Community and Junior Colleges
   One Dupont Circle
   Washington, DC 20036

American Association of University Professors
   1012 Fourteenth Street NW
   Washington, DC 20005

American Federation of Teachers
   555 New Jersey Avenue NW
   Washington, DC 20001

National Association of Professional Educators
   412 First Street SE
   Washington, DC 20003

National Education Association
   1201 Sixteenth Street NW
   Washington, DC 20036

CHAPTER 8

ENVIRONMENTAL ORGANIZATIONS

During the last quarter century, new conservation and environmental groups have sprung up like toadstools after evening dew. What with acid rain, the greenhouse effect, ozone depletion, polluted air over our cities, depletion of ground water reserves, to say nothing of the destruction of rain forests, fouling of ocean floors, toxic poisons in the soil, and threats from nuclear power plants, these organizations have assumed an ever-increasing importance in calling attention to such threats as well as taking firm action to solve some of the problems. Unfortunately, however, these nonprofit groups offer comparatively few job opportunities to those eager to enter this vital field.

In 1990, 44 percent of the foresters and conservation scientists worked for the federal government, 26 percent for state governments, 7 percent for local governments, and most of the balance for private industry, or they were self-employed. Nevertheless, in order to provide some information about the extremely limited environmental and conservation jobs that may be available from time to time with nonprofit organizations, we present the following brief information for those interested in considering a career in this field, be it with government, industry, or a nonprofit group.

Foresters manage timberland, supervise planting and growing of new trees, regulate timber sales.

Range managers (also called conservationists, ecologists, scientists) manage, improve, and protect rangelands in order to get the greatest use without damaging the environment.

Soil conservationists provide technical assistance to farmers, ranchers, and others concerned with conservation of soil, water, and other natural resources.

Planners study all aspects of a certain problem or goal and devise methods to accomplish the purpose or project.

Starting annual salaries in the federal government for the above positions averaged $17,000 (1991). Educational requirements would be a minimum of a bachelor's degree in forestry, range management, soil science, economics, or allied subjects. Many colleges and universities offer programs in environmental studies, which prepare students for specialized jobs. You will find descriptions of these in college catalogs on file at your school guidance office or in your public library. Obviously, the more education you have, the better the position and salary you can expect to obtain.

For the following positions the minimum educational requirement is a two-year associate degree from a community college or vocational/technical school or college, although a four-year degree would be preferable. Salary figures are for the late 1980s.

Environmental control technicians (also called pollution control technicians) are responsible for field investigations and other programs to discover means of controlling or eliminating ground water pollution. They may also specialize in air, light, and noise pollution control. Average annual salary, $25,000.

Soil conservation technicians help develop conservation plans for woodlands, open fields, management of water resources, use of cover crops. Average annual salary, $11,000 to $18,000.

Conservation planners work with property owners and others to plan reforestation, crop usage, drainage, need for water controls. Average annual salary, $15,000 to $22,000.

In addition to the national nonprofit organizations listed at the end of this chapter, in your state there probably are a number of local chapters of these groups as well as independent conservation and environmental societies. Examples of the latter include: The Vermont Natural Resources Council, Save the Redwoods League, the Society for the Preservation of New Hampshire's Forests, the League to Save Lake Tahoe, the Ozark Society, and the Columbia River Conservation League.

To locate some of these groups, look in the yellow pages of your telephone directory under the heading "Environmental, Conservation, and Ecological Organizations" or similar titles. Your local employment security office or public library may also be able to help you.

As is true throughout this book, the following organizations are thought to have large enough staffs to offer employment opportunities from time to time. You may also want to check the Gale *Encyclopedia of Associations* for names of organizations not listed here but that may especially interest you.

American Forestry Association
P. O. Box 2000
Washington, DC 20013

Conservation Foundation
1250 Twenty-fourth Street NW
Washington, DC 20037

Ducks Unlimited
One Waterfowl Way
Long Grove, IL 60014

Friends of the Earth
530 Seventh Street SE
Washington, DC 20003

Greenpeace International
    436 U Street NW
    Washington, DC 20009

Izaak Walton League of America
    1401 Wilson Boulevard
    Arlington, VA 22209

National Association of Conservation Districts
    509 Capitol Court NE
    Washington, DC 20002

National Audubon Society
    950 Third Avenue
    New York, NY 10022

National Wildlife Federation
    1412 Sixteenth Street NW
    Washington, DC 20036

Nature Conservancy
    1815 North Lynn Street
    Arlington, VA 22209

Sierra Club
    730 Polk Street
    San Francisco, CA 94109

Society for Range Management
    1839 York Street
    Denver, CO 80206

Soil Conservation Society of America
    7515 NE Ankeny Road
    Ankeny, IA 50021

Wilderness Society
    900 Seventeenth Street NW
    Washington, DC 20006

World Wildlife Fund
    1250 Twenty-fourth Street NW
    Washington, DC 20037

CHAPTER 9

SPECIAL INTEREST GROUPS

In this chapter we have gathered those organizations that do not logically fit in any of the other parts of the book. As you will discover, they are quite diverse and one or two of them just possibly may open new career horizons for you. We hope that will be the case!

AUTOMOBILE CLUBS

Two automobile clubs offer members emergency road service and other motorist-related benefits. The AAA is the largest, with almost thirty million members and some thousand offices, which provide career opportunities for those who are automobile lovers, scattered about the nation.

The two principal clubs are:

American Automobile Association (AAA)
   1000 AAA Drive
   Heathrow, FL 32746

American Legal Association (ALA)
   888 Worcester Street
   Wellesley, MA 02181

CREDIT UNIONS

Credit unions date back to 1849 when Friedrich Raiffeisen, the mayor of a small German town, established a credit society to enable residents to avoid usurious interest rates and improve their standard of living. Thus, if people pooled their savings in their own bank, they could lend the money to each other at a low rate. The idea spread to the United States in 1907. Edward A. Filene, the wealthy Boston merchant and philanthropist, started organizing credit unions throughout the country. Since then the movement has spread and grown until today there are over twenty thousand company-sponsored and independent credit unions serving more than forty thousand members with assets well over $50 billion.

Because of staff turnover plus newly created positions, there are thousands of openings each year. Organizations need the usual office personnel including tellers, accountants, and other financial specialists as well as computer operators. Look in the yellow pages of your telephone directory under "Credit Unions" for the names of those near you. Contact the following for further information as well as a possible career opening:

Credit Union Executive Society
  P. O. Box 14167
  Madison, WI 53714

Credit Union National Association
  P. O. Box 431
  Madison, WI 53701

National Association of Federal Credit Unions
  P. O. Box 3769
  Washington, DC 20007

FRATERNAL SOCIETIES

As de Tocqueville noted, Americans love to form and join organizations. In the extreme we find the Burlington Liars' Club, the International Twins Association, and the Procrastinators' Club of America. On the much more serious end of the spectrum, many fraternal societies started during the nineteenth and early twentieth centuries among European ethnic groups who came to the United States. They settled in large cities where they were lonely and found it difficult to make a living. Many of these groups formed societies to provide a place where friends and relatives could meet and also operate their own financial company, which offered low-cost insurance to members. Since then most of these groups have grown and today several exist primarily as insurance underwriters within the framework of the original fraternal organization. In addition, other fraternal groups have originated for various purposes, some solely for fraternal reasons, and often these groups have elected to undertake worthwhile continuing charitable activities.

All of the groups listed below have sizable headquarters staffs and may offer possible careers. If you are interested in any of them, write to the personnel department and ask for employment information.

Association Canada Americaine
    P. O. Box 989
    Manchester, NH 03105

Benevolent and Protective Order of Elks
    2750 Lake View Avenue
    Chicago, IL 60614

Catholic Aid Association
    3499 Lexington Avenue North
    St. Paul, MN 55112

Catholic Association of Foresters
    347 Commonwealth Avenue
    Boston, MA 02115

Catholic Family Life Insurance
    P. O. Box 11563
    Milwaukee, WI 53211

Catholic Knights Insurance Society
  1100 West Wells Street
  Milwaukee, WI 53233

Catholic Order of Foresters
  P. O. Box 3012
  Naperville, IL 60566

Croation Fraternal Union of America
  100 Delaney Drive
  Pittsburgh, PA 15235

General Federation of Women's Clubs
  1734 N Street NW
  Washington, DC 20036

Imperial Council of the Ancient Arabic Order of the Nobles of the
    Mystic Shrine for North America (Masons)
  P. O. Box 31356
  Tampa, FL 33631

Independent Order of Foresters
  789 Don Mills Road
  Don Mills, Ontario, Canada M3C 1T9

Independent Order of Odd Fellows
  422 North Trade Street
  Winston-Salem, NC 27101

Japanese American Citizens League
  1765 Sutter Street
  San Francisco, CA 94115

Knights of Columbus
  Columbus Plaza
  New Haven, CT 06507

Knights Templar, Grand Encampment, U.S.A.
  14 East Jackson Boulevard
  Chicago, IL 60604

Loyal Order of the Moose
  Mooseheart, IL 60539

Modern Woodmen of America
  Mississippi and 117th Street
  Rock Island, IL 61201

National Association of Arab Americans
  2033 M Street NW
  Washington, DC 20036

National Catholic Society of Foresters
  446 East Ontario Street
  Chicago, IL 60611

Order of United Commercial Travelers of America
  632 North Park Street
  Columbus, OH 43215

Rosicrucian Order
  Rosicrucian Park
  San Jose, CA 95191

Sons of Norway
  1455 West Lake Street
  Minneapolis, MN 55408

Woodman of the World Life Insurance Society
  1700 Farnam Street
  Omaha, NE 68102

GENEALOGICAL SOCIETIES

Increasing numbers of Americans are becoming interested in genealogy, and genealogical societies are appearing throughout the country. Most of them have volunteer staffs, but you may find a few that can afford a paid employee or two. Mention should be made of the comprehensive genealogical register of the entire country being compiled by the Church of Jesus Christ of the Latter Day Saints at their headquarters in Salt Lake City, Utah. The following are the two major genealogical societies you might contact if this subject intrigues you.

New England Historic Genealogical Society
   101 Newbury Street
   Boston, MA 02116

New York Genealogical and Biographical Society
   122 East Fifty-eighth Street
   New York, NY 10022

LABOR UNIONS

The first labor union in this country is thought to be that started in 1792 by a group of shoemaker journeymen in Philadelphia. Two hundred years later, some 16,746,000 men and women belonged to labor unions, comprising 16.1 percent of the labor force. Both their headquarters and regional offices offer job opportunities, one of the most interesting being that of union organizer. For further employment information, write one or more of the following organizations.

Air Line Pilots Association, International
   1625 Massachusetts Avenue NW
   Washington, DC 20036

Amalgamated Clothing and Textile Workers Union
   15 Union Square West
   New York, NY 10003

American Federation of Labor (AFL)
   815 Sixteenth Street NW
   Washington, DC 20036

American Federation of State, County, and Municipal Employees
   1625 L Street NW
   Washington, DC 20036

American Federation of Teachers
   555 New Jersey Avenue NW
   Washington, DC 20001

American Postal Workers Union
1300 L Street NW
Washington, DC 20005

Association of Flight Attendants
1625 Massachusetts Avenue NW
Washington, DC 20036

Civil Service Employees Association
143 Washington Avenue
Albany, NY 12210

International Brotherhood of Teamsters, Chauffeurs, Warehousemen
and Helpers of America
25 Louisiana Avenue NW
Washington, DC 20001

International Chemical Workers Union
1655 West Market Street
Akron, OH 44313

International Woodworkers of America
25 Cornell
Gladstone, OR 97027

National Air Traffic Controllers Association
444 North Capitol Street NW
Washington, DC 20001

National Association of American School Employees and Retirees
13902 Robson Street
Detroit, MI 48227

National Education Association
1201 Sixteenth Street NW
Washington, DC 20036

National Treasury Employees Union
1730 K Street NW
Washington, DC 20036

Sailors Union of the Pacific
450 Harrison Street
San Francisco, CA 94105

United Farm Workers of America
  Box 62-La Paz
  Keene, CA 93531

United Food and Commercial Workers International Union
  1775 K Street NW
  Washington, DC 20006

United Paperworkers International Union
  P. O. Box 1475
  Nashville, TN 37202

United Steelworkers of America
  Five Gateway Center
  Pittsburgh, PA 15222

MILITARY-RELATED AND PATRIOTIC SOCIETIES

Due to the size of the office staffs of the organizations listed below, they offer possible job opportunities to those interested in working for these causes. Except for the patriotic Daughters of the American Revolution, the other societies concentrate their efforts on improving their members' welfare in one way or another.

Air Forces Relief and Benefit Association
  909 North Washington Street
  Alexandria, VA 22313

American Legion
  P. O. Box 1055
  Indianapolis, IN 46204

Army and Air Force Mutual Aid Association
  Fort Meyer
  Arlington, VA 22211

Daughters of the American Revolution
  1776 D Street NW
  Washington, DC 20006

Disabled American Veterans
P. O. Box 14301
Cincinnati, OH 45250

Fleet Reserve Association
1303 New Hampshire Avenue NW
Washington, DC 20009

Jewish War Veterans of the U.S.A.
1811 R Street NW
Washington, DC 20009

Ladies Auxiliary to the Veterans of Foreign Wars of the United States
406 West Thirty-fourth Street
Kansas City, MO 64111

Navy Relief Society
801 North Randolph Street
Arlington, VA 22203

Retired Enlisted Association
14305 East Alameda Avenue
Aurora, CO 80012

Retired Officers Association
201 North Washington Street
Alexandria, VA 22314

Veterans of Foreign Wars of the United States
406 West Thirty-fourth Street
Kansas City, MO 64111

PERFORMING ARTS

Is your greatest dream to be standing before a symphony orchestra and choir, baton in hand, ready to conduct Handel's *Messiah?* Or is it to be gliding across the stage with your partner in the first performance of a new modern dance? Perhaps you visualize yourself in the leading role of a classical drama or as the star of an Academy Award-winning motion picture. Whatever your aspiration in some area of the performing arts, we would encourage you to hold on to that dream, but be prepared to accept a lesser role.

The sad fact is that there are comparatively few jobs for top performers, and that even though you have studied conscientiously and achieved recognition, to reach the top you must have that added "something," that rare extra talent or spark, which most of us lack. You must have it to achieve a successful career in some branch of the performing arts.

Don't give up, though! Continue to play that piano, dance, participate in amateur theatricals. There may well be outlets in your community where you can use your talents as an avocation, not a vocation. Remember, it is always possible that you might take the giant step forward later!

You might consider working for national organizations, such as those listed below, representing the artists in your area of interest. This will enable you to rub shoulders with top performers and carve out a career in your chosen field, although it may not be what you envisioned for yourself. Nevertheless, who knows what such a job might lead to, what doors it might open, what adventures and excitement it might bring, whom you might meet, or what sudden surprise may await you!

Earnings statistics are not available for any of the positions in these nonprofit organizations. However, entry-level jobs in clerical or other office-related jobs would undoubtedly be similar to prevailing wages for these positions in other areas. The important thing is to get started!

American Conservatory Theatre Foundation
  450 Geary Street
  San Francisco, CA 94102

American Film Institute
  1180 Avenue of the Americas
  New York, NY 10036

American Guild of Organists
475 Riverside Drive
New York, NY 10115

American Music Festival Association
2323 West Lincoln Avenue
Anaheim, CA 92801

American Place Theatre
111 West Forty-sixth Street
New York, NY 10036

American Symphony Orchestra League
777 Fourteenth Street NW
Washington, DC 20005

Anthology Film Archives
32 Second Avenue
New York, NY 10003

Ballet Theatre Foundation
890 Broadway
New York, NY 10003

Broadcast Music Inc.
320 West Fifty-seventh Street
New York, NY 10019

Chamber Music America
545 Eighth Avenue
New York, NY 10018

Circus Education Specialists, Inc.
67 Lion Lane
Westbury, NY 11590

Country Music Foundation
4 Music Square East
Nashville, TN 37203

Dramatists Guild
234 West Forty-fourth Street
New York, NY 10036

Drum Corps International
  P. O. Box 548
  Lombard, IL 60148

Eugene O'Neill Memorial Theatre Center
  305 Great Neck Road
  Waterford, CT 06385

League of American Theatres and Producers
  226 West Forty-seventh Street
  New York, NY 10036

Metropolitan Opera Association
  Lincoln Center
  New York, NY 10023

Metropolitan Opera Guild
  70 Lincoln Center Plaza
  New York, NY 10023

Opera America
  777 Fourteenth Street NW
  Washington, DC 20005

Society for the Preservation of and Enjoyment of Barber Shop
    Quartet Singing in America
  6315 Third Avenue
  Kenosha, WI 53143

Theatre Communications Group
  355 Lexington Avenue
  New York, NY 10017

Theatre Development Fund
  1501 Broadway
  New York, NY 10036

Theatre Guild
  226 West Forty-seventh Street
  New York, NY 10036

Young Concert Artists
  250 West Fifty-seventh Street
  New York, NY 10019

Young Filmmakers Foundation
817 Broadway
New York, NY 10003

RELIGIOUS CAREERS

Since every reader of this book either has his or her own religious belief or is an agnostic or atheist, we must recognize an important fact. Each individual is probably interested only in the religious denomination or sect of which he or she is a member and is not likely to seek a career with a group outside his or her own. One's religion is a very personal affair.

Accordingly it is our recommendation that if you are interested in a career in some aspect of your religious faith, be it as a religious leader or in some other occupation, you talk with your minister, priest, rabbi, or spiritual leader. There are so many religions and headquarters offices, it would be impractical if not impossible to list them here for those seeking a position in one of them. You can obtain the name and address of your church's headquarters from the spiritual leader or the church office.

If you are thinking of preparing to become a minister, priest, rabbi, or spiritual leader of a particular denomination or sect, you may find that there is more than one educational path to your goal. Your training may depend on how much time you can afford to put into schooling, the educational facilities available to you, and the minimum requirements you must meet to achieve your goal.

In the Protestant ministry, many denominations require or prefer a bachelor's degree followed by study at a theological school. However, some denominations and sects have no formal educational requirements, and others accept candidates who have trained in a Bible college, Bible institute, or liberal arts college. Those who hope to be Orthodox rabbis will find some thirty-five seminaries to choose from and must study from four to six years. Preparation for the priesthood may be done at one of the some 230 seminaries that require eight years of training following high school. (Seminaries never deny an applicant admission because of a lack of funds.)

In the average small church or synagogue, the members volunteer their services for all or most of the administrative positions. Larger institutions may employ a secretary, custodian, and even an administrator. Organists are usually paid, and in more affluent churches the choir director and soloists may be salaried.

As previously mentioned, for advice and help in discussing your career plans, start by consulting your spiritual leader.

The following organizations are nondenominational and may interest you because of their different purposes:

American Bible Society
    1865 Broadway
    New York, NY 10023

National Conference of Christians and Jews
    71 Fifth Avenue
    New York, NY 10003

National Ecumenical Coalition
    4300 Old Dominion Drive
    Arlington, VA 22207

Religion in American Life
    2 Queenston Place
    Princeton, NJ 08540

SCIENCE, TECHNOLOGY, AND ENGINEERING

Let's face it. There are few positions in nonprofit organizations for engineers and scientists. Industry and government are the dominant employers, although colleges and universities also employ a few in teaching and research capacities. The minimum educational requirement for a professional position is a college degree, but many men and women who seek to qualify for new technology and enhance their earnings take graduate degrees. Training in a vocational/technical school or two-year college course will also qualify you for certain subprofessional positions from which it is possible to advance. Of course, you can always return to college to obtain further education in your field.

There are numerous engineering and scientific organizations that offer extremely limited employment to college-trained men and women. They also hire the usual clerical staff and administrative employees. The following list will give you a broad choice of specialized nonprofit organizations that service their membership and promote their welfare.

American Association for the Advancement of Science
1333 H Street NW
Washington, DC 20005

American Chemical Society
1155 Sixteenth Street NW
Washington, DC 20036

American Forestry Association
P. O. Box 2000
Washington, DC 20013

American Geophysical Union
2000 Florida Avenue NW
Washington, DC 20009

American Institute of Aeronautics and Astronautics
370 L'Enfant Promenade SW
Washington, DC 20024

American Institute of Biological Sciences
730 Eleventh Street NW
Washington, DC 20001

American Institute of Mining, Metallurgical and Petroleum Engineers
345 East Forty-seventh Street
New York, NY 10017

American Institute of Physics
   335 East Forty-fifth Street
   New York, NY 10017

American Meteorological Society
   45 Beacon Street
   Boston, MA 01208

American Nuclear Society
   555 North Kensington Avenue
   LaGrange, IL 60525

American Society of Agricultural Engineers
   2950 Niles Road
   St. Joseph, MI 49085

American Society of Civil Engineers
   345 East Forty-seventh Street
   New York, NY 10017

American Society of Heating, Refrigerating, and Air-Conditioning
      Engineers
   1791 Tullie Circle NE
   Atlanta, GA 30329

American Society of Safety Engineers
   1800 East Oakton Street
   Des Plaines, IL 60016

ASM (Metallurgy) International
   Materials Park, OH 44073

Association of Ground Water Scientists and Engineers
   6375 Riverside Drive
   Dublin, OH 43017

Institute of Electrical and Electronics Engineers
   345 East Forty-seventh Street
   New York, NY 10017

Institute of Industrial Engineers
   25 Technology Park/Atlanta
   Norcross, GA 30092

Instrument Society of America
P. O. Box 12277
Research Triangle Park, NC 27709

National Academy of Sciences
2101 Constitution Avenue NW
Washington, DC 20418

National Bureau of Economic Research
1050 Massachusetts Avenue
Cambridge, MA 02138

National Space Society
922 Pennsylvania Avenue SE
Washington, DC 20003

Optical Society of America
1819 Jefferson Place NW
Washington, DC 20036

SAE (Society of Automotive Engineers)
400 Commonwealth Drive
Warrendale, PA 15096

Society of Petroleum Engineers
P. O. Box 833836
Richardson, TX 75083

Society of Plastics Engineers
14 Fairfield Drive
Brookfield, CT 06805

CHAPTER 10

HOBBIES AND SPORTS

HOBBIES

What is your hobby or special interest? Collecting stamps, bridge, football, training dogs, gardening, collecting dolls, tennis, making and flying model planes, chess, baseball? Believe it or not, you might be able to turn your avocation (hobby or other interest) into a vocation (profession or occupation). Although this is not true for the majority of hobbies, there are some that offer limited career possibilities for those who have a serious interest in them.

A word of caution: for many of us the skill we acquire such as painting, singing, writing, sculpturing, acting, should be enjoyed for the personal satisfaction one experiences from the activity, and it should not be directed toward earning a living. It all depends upon the individual, and although one may derive great pleasure from a hobby, nevertheless it may prove impossible to turn this avocation into a vocation or profession. That is because the individual lacks that special extra aptitude or drive required to become professional.

There are few nonprofit hobby organizations that offer job opportunities, but readers who have a genuine interest in their avocation, and wish at least to explore the idea of turning it into a career, should investigate the possibilities. The usual organization has one or two employees who may or may not be salaried. The headquarters may be located in the home of the association's president or secretary. However, don't let this discourage you. Pursue every lead and possibility since there are some groups that employ a number of men and women and you might well find a beginning job that leads to a career.

If your interest is not represented in the following list, check the Gale *Encyclopedia of Associations,* and if unsuccessful, ask your library's reference librarian to help you.

Academy of Model Aeronautics
1910 Samuel Morse Drive
Reston, VA 22090

American Contract Bridge League
2990 Airways
Memphis, TN 38132

American Horticultural Society
7931 East Boulevard Drive
Alexandria, VA 22308

American Institute of Wine and Food
1550 Bryant Street
San Francisco, CA 94103

American Kennel Club
51 Madison Avenue
New York, NY 10010

American Numismatic Society
Broadway and 155th Street
New York, NY 10032

American Philatelic Society
100 Oakwood Avenue
State College, PA 16803

American Radio Relay League
225 Main Street
Newington, CT 06111

American Shortwave Listeners Club
16182 Ballad Lane
Huntington Beach, CA 92649

Cat Fanciers' Association
1309 Allaire Avenue
Ocean, NJ 07712

Confederate Air Force
Box CAF
Harlingen, TX 78551

Family Motor Coach Association
8291 Clough
Cincinnati, OH 45244

Gold Wing Road Riders Association
3035 West Thomas Road
Phoenix, AZ 85017

National Association of Watch and Clock Collectors
514 Poplar Street
Columbus, PA 17512

National Council of State Garden Clubs
4401 Magnolia Avenue
St. Louis, MO 83110

National Gardening Association
180 Flynn Avenue
Burlington, VT 05401

National Street Rod Association
4030 Park Avenue
Memphis, TN 38111

Sports Car Club of America
9033 East Easter Place
Englewood, CO 80112

United Kennel Club
100 East Kilgore Road
Kalamazoo, MI 49001

United States Chess Federation
186 Route 9W
New Windsor, NY 12553

Writers Guild of America
8955 Beverly Boulevard
West Hollywood, CA 90048

SPORTS

This section should excite you if you are a sports enthusiast and would like to find a career in the field that especially interests you.

"But I'm not good enough to be a professional player," you may well protest. "What kind of work could I ever find in the athletic arena?"

Your answer may be found in the list of sports organizations listed below, as well as in many other smaller ones, which are not included here. Thus, because of your firsthand knowledge of a particular activity, you might find an opening in an administrative office and gradually work your way up. Most head offices employ a wide variety of employees, which could include some or all of the following: clerical workers such as file clerks, typists, and secretaries; public relations staff members; writers; or scouts who find new players—the possibilities may surprise you.

Before you start looking for one of these jobs, if you think that you have what it takes to become a professional player, discuss your goal with your school or college coach or the head of the athletic department. He or she should be able to evaluate your potential, give helpful advice, and steer you in the right direction.

However, if becoming a baseball, hockey, football, tennis, or other star is out of the question, contact the personnel manager at the headquarters of your favorite sport and ask how you might qualify for a position on the staff. Although there may not be any openings when you inquire, explain your eagerness to become associated with the organization and ask how you might best qualify yourself to join the staff. If after you have acquired the necessary skill for a particular job and there is still no opening, find a position elsewhere and ask the sports organization's personnel manager to contact you when an opening occurs so you may make a formal application. Although this will not guarantee you a job, it will surely indicate your sincere interest and ensure you will be given serious consideration for a position.

Some sports organizations have so few dues-paying members they are operated from the president's or secretary's home to save office expense. Others that have small staffs are not listed below either, but they should be contacted if you are making an intensive job search. Your best source for this information is the Athletic and Sports Organizations section of the *Encyclopedia of Associations.*

Sports fans will recognize many of the organizations listed here, and although they are nonprofit, those who play on the teams or work in the offices are salaried. In some cases the players make more than many presidents of major corporations!

Adirondack Mountain Club
  RR#3 Box 3055
  Lake George, NY 12845

Amateur Hockey Association of the United States
  2997 Broadmoor Valley Road
  Colorado Springs, CO 80906

Amateur Trapshooting Association
  601 West National Road
  Vandalia, OH 45377

American Bowling Congress
  5301 South Seventy-sixth Street
  Greendale, WI 53129

American Camping Association
5000 State Road 67N
Martinsville, IN 46151

American Hockey League
218 Memorial Avenue
West Springfield, MA 01089

American Horse Shows Association
220 East Forty-second Street
New York, NY 10017

American Lawn Bowls Association
8710 Tern Avenue
Fountain Valley, CA 92708

American Motorcyclist Association
33 Collegeview Road
Westerville, OH 43081

American Power Boat Association
P. O. Box 377
East Detroit, MI 48021

American Water Ski Association
799 Overlook Drive
Winter Haven, FL 33884

American Youth Soccer Organization
P. O. Box 5045
Hawthorne, CA 90251

Appalachian Mountain Club
5 Joy Street
Boston, MA 02108

Appalachian Trail Conference
P. O. Box 807
Harpers Ferry, WV 25425

Athletic Congress of the U.S.A.
1 Hoosier Drive
Indianapolis, IN 46225

Babe Ruth Baseball
  P. O. Box 5000
  Trenton, NJ 08638

Big Ten Conference
  1111 Plaza Drive
  Schaumburg, IL 60173

Boat Owners Association of the United States
  8805 Pickett Street
  Alexandria, VA 22304

Championship Auto Racing Teams
  390 Enterprise Court
  Bloomfield Hills, MI 48013

Christian Camping International/U.S.A.
  P. O. Box 646
  Wheaton, IL 60189

International Baseball Association
  201 South Capitol Avenue
  Indianapolis, IN 46225

International Cheerleading Foundation
  10660 Barkley
  Overland Park, KS 66212

International Hot Rod Association
  P. O. Box 8018
  Waco, TX 76714

Jockey Club
  40 East Fifty-second Street
  New York, NY 10022

Jockey's Guild
  20 East Forty-sixth Street
  New York, NY 10017

Ladies Professional Golf Association
  4675 Sweetwater Boulevard
  Sugar Land, TX 77479

League of American Wheelmen
  6707 Whitestone Road
  Baltimore, MD 21207

Little League Baseball
  P. O. Box 3485
  Williamsport, PA 17701

The Mountaineers
  300 Third Avenue West
  Seattle, WA 98119

Naismith Memorial Basketball Hall of Fame
  P. O. Box 179
  Springfield, MA 01101

National Association for Stock Car Auto Racing
  P. O. Box 2875
  Daytona Beach, FL 32115

National Association of Intercollegiate Athletics
  1221 Baltimore
  Kansas City, MO 64105

National Association of Professional Baseball Leagues
  P. O. Box A
  St. Petersburg, FL 33731

National Association of Underwater Instructors
  P. O. Box 14650
  Montclair, CA 91763

National Bicycle League
  P. O. Box 729
  Dublin, OH 43017

National Collegiate Athletic Association
  P. O. Box 1906
  Mission, KS 66201

National Dance-Exercise Instructors Training Association
  1503 South Washington Avenue
  Minneapolis, MN 55454

National Football League Players Association
  2021 L Street NW
  Washington, DC 20036

National Handicapped Sports
  1145 Nineteenth Street NW
  Washington, DC 20036

National Horseshoe Pitchers Association of America
  P. O. Box 278
  Munroe Falls, OH 44262

National Hot Rod Association
  2035 Financial Way
  Glendora, CA 91740

National Rifle Association
  1600 Rhode Island Avenue NW
  Washington, DC 20036

National Skeet Shooting Association
  P. O. Box 680007
  San Antonio, TX 78268

National Strength and Conditioning Association
  P. O. Box 81410
  Lincoln, NE 68501

National Youth Sports Coaches Association
  2611 Old Okeechobee Road
  West Palm Beach, FL 33409

North American Hunting Club
  P. O. Box 3401
  Minnetonka, MN 55343

New York Road Runners Club
  9 East Eighty-ninth Street
  New York, NY 10128

People to People Sports Committee
  80 Cutter Mill Road
  Great Neck, NY 11021

Professional Golfers Association of America
P. O. Box 10960
Palm Beach Gardens, FL 33418

Professional Rodeo Cowboys Association
101 Prorodeo Drive
Colorado Springs, CO 80919

Soaring Society of America
P. O. Box E
Hobbs, NM 88241

Southeastern Conference
3000 Galleria Tower
Birmingham, AL 35244

Special Olympics International
1350 New York Avenue NW
Washington, DC 20005
(for the disabled)

Sport Fishing Institute
1010 Massachusetts Avenue NW
Washington, DC 20001

United States Amateur Confederation of Roller Skating
P. O. Box 6579
Lincoln, NE 68506

United States Auto Club
4910 North Sixteenth Street
Indianapolis, IN 46224

United States Cycling Federation
1750 East Boulder Street
Colorado Springs, CO 80909

United States Equestrian Team
Gladstone, NJ 07934

United States Field Hockey Association
1750 East Boulder Street
Colorado Springs, CO 80909

United States Football Association
   1317 Washington Avenue
   Golden, CO 80401

United States Golf Association
   P. O. Box 708
   Far Hills, NJ 07931

United States Gymnastics Federation
   2015 Capitol
   Indianapolis, IN 46225

United States Olympic Committee
   1750 East Boulder Street
   Colorado Springs, CO 80909

United States Parachute Association
   1440 Duke Street
   Alexandria, VA 22314

United States Ski Association
   P. O. Box 100
   Park City, UT 84060

United States Soccer Federation
   1750 East Boulder Street
   Colorado Springs, CO 80909

United States Swimming, Inc.
   1750 East Boulder Street
   Colorado Springs, CO 80909

United States Tennis Association
   1212 Avenue of the Americas
   New York, NY 10036

United States Trotting Association
   750 Michigan Avenue
   Columbus, OH 43215

United States Yacht Racing Union
   P. O. Box 209
   Newport, RI 02840

U.S.A. Amateur Boxing Foundation
  1750 East Boulder Street
  Colorado Springs, CO 80909

U.S.A. Wrestling
  225 South Academy Boulevard
  Colorado Springs, CO 80910

Women's International Bowling Congress
  5301 South Seventy-sixth Street
  Greenville, WI 53129

Yachting Club of America
  P. O. Box 11250
  Ft. Lauderdale, FL 33339

Young American Bowling Alliance
  5301 South Seventy-sixth Street
  Greenville, WI 53129

EARNINGS SUMMARY

Although no information is available on earnings in hobby-related organizations or the headquarters offices of various athletic groups, players' salaries—especially those in the high numbers—are often revealed in the newspapers. If you hope to find employment with one of the organizations listed in this chapter, your entry-level job will probably be of a clerical nature so that the salary data at the end of the first chapter may prove informative.

CHAPTER 11

CAREERS IN FUND-RAISING

Chances are when you see the words "fund-raising" in the paper or hear them on the news, they usually refer to political fund-raising. But fund-raising for America's million-plus non-profit organizations is a very different and even more challenging business since virtually all nonprofits depend vitally on tax-deductible charitable contributions for their continued operation and growth. The National Society of Fund-Raising Executives defines fund-raising as "the seeking of gifts from various sources as conducted by 501(c) (3) [non-profit] organizations" and describes a fund-raiser as "one who makes his or her living from working as a member of an organization's or institution's development department, as an independent fund-raising consultant, or as a member of a fund-raising consulting firm."

Fund-raising has played a central role in America's life since colonial days, when the first settlers found they had to rely upon themselves, not government, to provide schools, churches, public meeting places, and infirmaries. Perhaps the first American fund-raisers were the three clergymen the Massachusetts Bay Colony sent back to England in 1640—just twenty years after the Pilgrims landed at Plymouth Rock—to raise money for Harvard College. They returned with five hundred pounds in contributions, a sizable sum of money in those times. Fund-raising in the United States focused primarily on higher education and religion until the 1800s, when these causes were joined by an ever-expanding range of health, civic, human services, and cultural organizations.

Historian Henry Steele Commager has pointed out that "Americans managed without energetic government for so long a time that they came to prefer voluntary public enterprise. If they wanted a college, they built one, and they kept right on doing that into the twentieth century. Because participation is the very essence of democracy, it is difficult to exaggerate the value of this aspect of American philanthropy."

The importance of fund-raising today is emphasized by the more than $125 billion in philanthropic contributions that United States nonprofits receive each year. Virtually all this income results directly or indirectly from the efforts of paid fund-raising professionals. Although most nonprofits receive the bulk of their funding from tuition, fees, tickets, memberships, and other sales, they nevertheless could not exist as we know them without the critical "margin for excellence" dollars they receive as a result of their fund-raising programs, whose sophistication, size, and effectiveness reflect their true importance.

There are two broad, intersecting avenues leading to careers in fund-raising. Today, nonprofits are establishing and expanding their own in-house fund-raising capabilities, usually referred to as the department of development or institutional advancement. Most of these institutions have had many years' experience in fund-raising, often working closely with those on the second career path—that is, professional fund-raising consultants, working for fund-raising consulting firms. Today, these companies are working increasingly on behalf of nonprofits, which are either new to sizable fund-raising programs or have less experience than those that have built their own full-blown development departments. If you were to conclude that this situation makes it possible to move back and forth from the institutional to the consulting sides (and back again), you would be correct. Not only do you have wide latitude of choice when you apply for your first job in fund-raising, you also have broader choices as your career advances. Many experienced fund-raising executives today, in fact, have spent some time on both sides of the desk.

FUND-RAISING TODAY

America's nonprofits meet essential public needs in education, health and medicine, social and human services, religion, and culture and the arts. Because they have at the heart of their service the mission to advance the public good, they are entitled to tax exemptions as 501(c) (3) institutions, meaning that they usually do not have to pay real estate or sales taxes and, most important from the standpoint of philanthropy and fund-raising, contributors can take deductions on their income tax reports for the money or property they donate.

A strong sense of dedication to advancing the common good is almost a prerequisite for a fulfilling, successful career in fund-raising. Yet, while the rewards of the work itself will undoubtedly be part of your overall compensation, pay levels in fund-raising, especially the more senior administrative and executive positions in large nonprofits such as hospitals and universities, have risen steadily, reflecting growing recognition of the importance to nonprofits of philanthropic income. In fund-raising consulting firms, pay advances have been less impressive, although experienced practitioners receive sizable salaries. Yet a "glass ceiling" exists for many fund-raising consultants and firms, the result both of strong competition among fund-raising consultants in a fairly crowded field, and the illogical perception of some nonprofits that fund-raising professionals should "give them a break." (Nonprofits rarely attempt to persuade other providers of professional services—attorneys, accountants, contractors, architects—to give them reduced rates!)

CURRENT TRENDS IN FUND-RAISING

As you consider a career in this field, you should be aware of a number of current trends in fund-raising, philanthropy, and the nonprofit world as a whole. As you read, do an informal check list of your own goals and expectations, your talents and resources, and your "personality" profile. In many cases, these will probably not be identical with those of friends who plan careers in business and the other professions.

Professional Training and Certification

The fund-raising business in recent years has made important strides toward becoming a true profession, like law or medicine, with a recognized body of knowledge and skills practitioners must master. Degree programs in fund-raising management are now offered by many colleges and universities. The National Society for Fund-Raising Executives (NSFRE) awards its CFRE diploma (Certified Fund-Raising Executive) to fund-raisers who can demonstrate wide knowledge of fund-raising and philanthropy and deep knowledge in certain central areas. This designation increasingly appears after the names of more and more fund-raising executives, many of them relatively young people only a year or two out of college. The Association for Healthcare Philanthropy offers a Fellows program along the same lines for fund-raisers specializing in hospital and medical institutions. (A list of fund-raising professional associations appears at the end of this chapter.)

Emphasis on Recruiting Women and Minorities

There is a strong trend toward hiring more women and minority group members among nonprofits' and consulting firms' fund-raising staff. Nonprofits have in fact traditionally had a commitment to equal opportunity employment and advancement opportunities. The growing numbers of women and minorities working in the field reflects this commitment as well as changes in society and nonprofits' programs and goals. They also reflect the recognition that increasingly women and minority group members are themselves serving on nonprofits' administrations and boards of trustees, and are, individually, also prospects for major philanthropic contributions and volunteer service.

Ability to Work as a Leader and a Follower

Large or "lead" gifts constitute the bulk of total funds raised during most capital fund-raising campaigns with as much as 80 percent of the goal coming from as few as 20 percent, or less, of the donors. This means that fund-raisers must be knowledgeable, confident, sensitive, and tactful in working with volunteers, both the individuals who donate their money and time to a cause, and the men and women (usually from the same group) who serve on nonprofits' boards of directors. Unlike the business world, where corporate directors seldom carry out the corporation's policies, volunteer leadership routinely plays a direct and active role in nonprofits' administration and management, and especially so in the important area of fund-raising.

Dedication Needed

As with most business or corporate jobs, if you set your sights on becoming a member of a nonprofit's or consulting firm's "professional" (i.e., executive) staff, you must be prepared to serve an apprenticeship during which you will gain exposure to a variety of situations and individuals. Willingness to travel extensively and work long hours, especially in the often hectic kickoff and conclusion of large capital campaigns, is a must. So are attention to personal appearance, dress, manners, speech and "body language," plus sensitivity to the particular environment in which you are working. A hospital, a medical center, a library, a Boy Scout chapter, a YMCA, a university, a small college, a national church organization, a battered women's shelter, a symphony orchestra, a dance company—each type of nonprofit has its own distinctive culture, which you must be able to recognize and fit into to be successful in your work as a fund-raising professional and in your efforts to advance your own career.

Practical Skills and Knowledge

Today it is assumed that virtually everyone reading this book will be computer literate, have basic typing/word processing skills, and will keep well informed about local, regional, national, and world events. You will need this background when you work to persuade large numbers of people, including individuals of prominence and wealth, to do what most of us find most difficult: give away large quantities of our money, commit large stretches of our time, and ask one's peers and friends to do the same. In working "behind the scenes" helping prepare the information and materials your volunteer leaders will require in these efforts, your information must be comprehensive, current, and accurate. The fund-raiser's "bible" is *Giving USA,* an annual report on philanthropy published by the AAFRC Trust for Philanthropy (address at end of chapter). This book should be on every fund-raiser's desk, providing as it does a very wide array of information critical to fund-raising success for all nonprofits, donors and volunteers, and all fund-raisers.

Ethics

Mirroring our society at large, nonprofits have increasingly become concerned with ethics in recent years. Fund-raisers at all levels and in all kinds of fund-raising programs must have high ethical and moral standards, since their duties will bring them into close contact with individuals and information who and which must be treated with appropriate confidentiality. Honesty and accuracy are also essential, as large sums of money are routinely handled by fund-raising personnel in an environment with fewer checks and balances than are typically found in the corporate world.

Careers in Fund-Raising

One of the most attractive things about the fund-raising profession is that you can "transfer" a great deal of experience gained in other jobs directly to nonprofit development. Public relations, teaching, marketing, advertising, journalism, research, communications—as well as work within or on behalf of institutions ranging from churches and missions, to hospitals and national health organizations, colleges and universities, secondary schools, museums, libraries, Y's, and Salvation Army chapters— will all provide you with a range of transferable experience and knowledge that, used wisely, can help make you a desirable candidate for a fund-raising position on either side of the desk. Today there is greater movement than ever before within nonprofits, from nonprofits to fund-raising firms and back again, as well as in and out of wholly different professions and jobs. Let us now look at the primary fund-raising "job descriptions" to get an overview of the field today.

JOBS IN NONPROFIT INSTITUTIONS AND ORGANIZATIONS

The vice president of development leads the organization's fund-raising efforts. He or she may supervise a department with as many as twenty or more employees, or work virtually as a one-person band or with an assistant and a secretary. The vice president/director usually reports to the organization's president or executive director, and typically works closely with the board of trustees from whose ranks emerge top volunteer leadership and major philanthropic support. Activities include planning and carrying out the institution's fund-raising efforts ranging from big-gift fund-raising in a capital campaign, to deferred gifts and bequests, annual giving, alumni, parent and grateful patient drives, plus the nonprofit's own employees.

Most nonprofits, in addition to their ongoing fund-raising programs, periodically conduct comprehensive capital campaigns that seek funds for such needs as major new construction and physical plant renovation; increasing the endowment to provide additional income for scholarships, named faculty chairs, and fellowships; and other ways of enhancing the institution's ability to compete with its peers for market share—students, patients, audiences (the fee incomes from which, in turn, are essential to the nonprofit's fiscal health). Goals for capital campaigns can range from $100,000 to $1,000,000, to as much as hundreds of millions, and even over $1 billion. In the case of most big-goal, multiyear campaigns, the vice president/director of development often hires additional specialized staff to work largely or exclusively on the capital campaign. In many cases, the nonprofit will decide to call upon a fund-raising consulting firm to help plan and carry out the campaign, usually utilizing in-house staff as well as personnel provided by the consultant such as a campaign director who, while employed by the firm, establishes his or her office in the development department or the campaign headquarters for the duration of the campaign. Consultants usually are able to offer a wide range of services and can provide communications, direct mail, deferred giving, and other specialists to head up special programs within the campaign and work with the nonprofit's staff.

The vice president/director of development is also responsible
directly or by delegation for hiring and supervising the development office staff, filling the following functions with individuals
who either report directly to him or her, or to one or more assistant
vice presidents/directors: annual giving*; deferred giving and
bequests; special events*; public relations; communications*;
marketing (often development office functions with regard to
marketing are integrated with institution-wide efforts in the same
areas); direct mail; data processing*; financial and gift control
procedures; and federal and other public grantsmanship. In addition, the vice president/director hires an office manager whose
support staff of secretaries*, computer/data processing personnel*, and others report to the office manager.

Among the requirements for this critical position are at least a
bachelor's degree, several years experience in nonprofit fund-
raising and administration, and strong planning, management,
and communications skills. There is a steady demand for such
individuals, and salaries are competitive with many equivalent
for-profit positions, especially among large hospital and medical
centers, major universities, national health and human services,
and arts and cultural institutions. Salary levels vary rather widely
by institution type, size, and location—a range from $25,000 to
$35,000 at the low end to as much as $125,000 and more at the
high end is not unusual. The median level would be roughly in
the area of $45,000 to $65,000. Recent compensation studies by
NAHD and others in the nonprofit hospital field show clearly that
these nonprofits (like many others) are also doing a good job of
equalizing compensation levels and advancement opportunities
for men and women performing the same work. The two most
common paths to the vice president/director are (1) rising through
the ranks of the institution's in-house fund-raising program, and

*Most usual avenues of entry to the profession.

(2) transferring from one nonprofit to a higher position at another institution with a large, more complex fund-raising program.

Assistant vice president/director of fund-raising positions are also demanding and provide excellent opportunities for career growth. Responsibilities can range from several employees to a narrower focus on one's own specialty and work. This position, whether there is one or several assistant vice presidents, can be a stepping stone to the top spot either within the same institution or at another, comparable nonprofit.

JOBS IN FUND-RAISING CONSULTING FIRMS

As with institutional development offices, fund-raising firms range in size from one-person operations to small concerns employing ten to twenty people, to full-service national companies with eighty or more employees. The most comprehensive listing of fund-raising consulting firms is the *Directory of Fund Raising Consultants,* published by The Taft Group (see list at end of chapter for addresses of principal organizations involved in fund-raising). The range and level of skills and experience required for a successful career in fund-raising with a consulting firm are essentially comparable to those for nonprofits. Indeed, there is a good deal of movement back and forth, by many fund-raisers, between the institutional and the consulting organizations.

Within the firms themselves, there is a typical corporate hierarchy of chairperson, president, secretary, treasurer, and usually a number of vice presidents as well as individuals working in administration (office management), data processing, research, secretarial, and often "internship" positions—an ideal way for college graduates who lack experience but want a career in fund-raising to break into the business. In addition, many firms have departments or individuals providing a variety of ancillary services ranging from data processing, computer applications, communications, writing and public relations, to deferred, annual, and other specialized giving programs.

As you would expect, the key to success for a consulting firm is sales and service, and by and large the people working in these areas command the highest salaries, aside from top administration. Although the terminology may vary from one firm to another, the two kinds of executive on which the company "marches" are the consulting senior officer (CSO) and the campaign director. The CSO is basically an account executive with responsibility for new business, sales, and supervision of services provided to clients. As the title implies, these people have considerable experience in the field, in-depth knowledge of fund-raising theory and practice, the personal skills required of a successful salesperson, and highly developed leadership and management skills. Campaign directors are assigned to a particular nonprofit client, and usually work on-site at the institution, often in their own office in the development or campaign office. They work closely with nonprofit professional fund-raising staff, as well as volunteer leadership including trustees. Frequently, these individuals serve as study directors prior to their firm being retained to provide campaign management. At this stage, working again with their CSO and the client's staff and volunteer leaders, they carry out planning, marketing, and feasibility studies to assess the levels and sources of potential support available to the organization via a capital campaign; identify prospective volunteer leaders and donors; and sharpen the focus of the nonprofit's case of rationale for significant financial support. Studies usually last from two to six months and typically entail a fair amount of travelling (unless the client is in the same city as the consulting firm and the employee concerned). Campaigns can last from six to eight months to three and even four or five years. Campaign management usually requires the campaign director to live on location full-time; most firms either defray living expenses directly or bill them to the client.

Compensation levels in fund-raising firms tend to be closely guarded information. Salary levels may be more, or less, than staff earn at the nonprofit they serve. Comparisons are also difficult to make because many individuals who work for consulting firms may do so on a part-time basis. For a cook's tour of the world of fund-raising, a few years' experience in a consulting firm can be invaluable and give you a broader perspective on the field as a whole than you would be likely to receive working in one nonprofit development office.

ENTRY-LEVEL JOBS

For people such as yourself, who probably will have little or no direct fund-raising experience, the positions indicated with an asterisk (*) on page 141 are the most usual avenues of opportunity, where some other skill you have or can develop quickly on the job can give you your first break into the field. We are talking here not about an individual who sees her-or himself as primarily as secretary, receptionist, data processor, or "guy/gal Friday" but a person who is seriously interested in building a career in fund-raising, starting with these basic skills. It is vital that you distinguish yourself as the second type at the outset, so nonprofit fund-raisers can identify you and give you opportunities to succeed as a part of their support and professional staff of tomorrow.

How can you best prepare yourself to convey that your interest is as much in the field itself as in the specific job? The answer is to make yourself as much of an expert as you can before you begin to apply and interview—on fund-raising, on nonprofits in general and the one(s) to which you are applying in particular, and on the community needs the nonprofit has identified as its target in setting forth its service mission.

Where can you find this information? The best place to start is to request a copy of the latest annual report from each nonprofit you are interested in. At the same time, check with your local library for books and publications on fund-raising, philanthropy, nonprofits, and the third sector, as nonprofits are sometimes called. If you are unable to find solid information in this manner, speak to your librarian and/or guidance counselor about the possibility of approaching one or more of the larger nonprofits (including community foundations) before you interview, to use some of their library materials.

What should you look for? *Giving USA,* referred to earlier in this chapter, is the "bible." In addition, be sure to read current and recent copies of *The Chronicle of Philanthropy* and other journals and reviews that may be available.

Another way to prepare is to work as a volunteer in one or more nonprofits whose programs interest you. Virtually all nonprofits need and welcome volunteers, from candystripers at hospitals, stack workers in libraries, readers to the blind, to tutors in your own or other schools. Ideally, you might work as a volunteer in local nonprofits' annual and other fund-raising efforts, which may range from helping cook and serve a turkey dinner or bringing meals to the housebound to manning the switchboard in phone-a-thons; selling tickets for performances, concerts, and drawings; and addressing envelopes for direct mail programs.

To find actual job opportunities, check your local papers' help wanted section under "Fund-Raisers and Development," as well as specific areas such as communications and writing in which you may have special skills. *The Chronicle of Philanthropy* lists job openings primarily for people with previous experience, but some of the descriptions can be useful in giving you a sense of the kinds of nonprofits in your community. Last but by no means least, check with employment agencies that specialize in fund-raising and/or marketing, communications, and public relations.

The principal organizations involved in various aspects of fund-raising follow:

American Association of Fund-Raising Counsel and the AAFRC Trust
for Philanthropy
25 West Forty-third Street
New York, NY 10036

Association for Healthcare Philanthropy
313 Park Avenue
Falls Church, VA 22046
(formerly National Association for Hospital Development)

The Foundation Center
79 Fifth Avenue
New York, NY 10003
(Maintains regional collections relating to fund-raising in public
libraries in Cleveland, San Francisco, and Washington, DC, in
addition to more than 175 cooperating collections throughout the
United States.)

The Fund-Raising School
Indiana University, Center on Philanthropy
850 West Michigan Street
Indianapolis, IN 46223

International Fund Raising Association
2425 North Central Expressway
Richardson, TX 75080

National Charities Information Bureau
19 Union Square West
New York, NY 10003

National Society of Fund Raising Executives
1101 King Street
Alexandria, VA 22314

National Voluntary Health Agencies
1660 L Street NW
Washington, DC 20036

United Way of America
701 North Fairfax Street
Alexandria, VA 22314

SUGGESTED READINGS

All of the following books are published by and available from VGM Career Horizons, 4255 West Touhy Avenue, Lincolnwood, IL 60646–1975.

Abbott, Marguerite. *Opportunities in Occupational Therapy Careers,* 1988.

Ahrens, Kathleen M. *Opportunities in Eye Care Careers,* 1991.

Banning, Kent. *Opportunities in Purchasing Careers,* 1990.

Basta, Nicholas. *Opportunities in Engineering Careers,* 1990.

Baxter, Neale J. *Opportunities in Counseling and Development Careers,* 1990.

Bekken, Bonnie B. *Opportunities in Performing Arts Careers,* 1991.

Bloch, Deborah P. *How to Get a Good Job and Keep It,* 1993.

———. *How to Have a Winning Job Interview,* 1992.

———. *How to Write a Winning Résumé,* 1989.

Bone, Jan. *Opportunities in Film Careers,* 1990.

Brown, Sheldon. *Opportunities in Biotechnology Careers,* 1989.

Cable, Fred B. *Opportunities in Pharmacy Careers,* 1990.

Caldwell, Carol Coles. *Opportunities in Nutrition Careers*, 1992.

Cardoza, Anne deSola. *Opportunities in Homecare Services Careers*, 1993.

Chmelynski, Carol C. *Opportunities in Food Services Careers*, 1992.

Donovan, Mary D. *Opportunities in Culinary Careers*, 1990.

Eberts, Marjorie and Margaret Gisler. *Careers for Good Samaritans and Other Humanitarian Types*, 1991.

———. *Careers for Culture Lovers and Other Artsy Types*, 1991.

Edelfelt, Roy. *Careers in Education*, 1993.

Ellis, Elmo I. *Opportunities in Broadcasting Careers*, 1992.

Ettinger, Blanche. *Opportunities in Office Occupations Careers*, 1989.

———. *Opportunities in Secretarial Careers*, 1992.

Fanning, Odom. *Opportunities in Environmental Careers*, 1991.

Fine, Janet. *Opportunities in Teaching Careers*, 1989.

Frederickson, Keville. *Opportunities in Nursing Careers*, 1989.

Garner, Geraldine O. *Careers in Social and Rehabilitation Services*, 1993.

Gerardi, Robert. *Opportunities in Music Careers*, 1991.

Heim, Kathleen. *Opportunities in Library and Information Science Careers*, 1992.

Heitzmann, Wm. Ray. *Careers for Sports Nuts and Other Athletic Types*, 1991.

———. *Opportunities in Marine and Maritime Careers*, 1988.

———. *Opportunities in Sports and Athletics Careers*, 1993.

Hoyt, Douglas B. *Opportunities in Information Systems Careers*, 1991.

Johnson, Bervin. *Opportunities in Photography Careers*, 1991.

Kacen, Alex. *Opportunities in Paramedical Careers,* 1989.

Karni, Karen R. *Opportunities in Medical Technology,* 1990.

Kendall, Bonnie. *Opportunities in Dental Care Careers,* 1991.

Kinney, Jane and Mike Fasulo. *Careers for Environmental Types and Others Who Respect the Earth,* 1993.

Krumhansl, Bernice R. *Opportunities in Physical Therapy Careers,* 1993.

Larkens, Patricia. *Opportunities in Speech-Language Pathology Careers,* 1988.

Maples, Wallace R. *Opportunities in Aerospace Careers,* 1991.

McAfee, Charles. *Opportunities in Psychology Careers,* 1988.

Miller, Louise. *Careers for Nature Lovers and Other Outdoor Types,* 1992.

Moore, Dick. *Opportunities in Acting Careers,* 1993.

Munday, Marianne F. *Opportunities in Crafts Careers,* 1993.

———. *Opportunities in Word Processing Careers,* 1991.

Nelson, John Oliver. *Opportunities in Religious Service Careers,* 1988.

Noerper, Norman. *Opportunities in Data Processing Careers,* 1989.

Paradis, Adrian A. *Opportunities in Cleaning Service Careers,* 1992.

———. *Resumes for Health and Medical Careers,* 1993.

Rosenberg, Martin. *Opportunities in Accounting Careers,* 1991.

Rotman, Morris B. *Opportunities in Public Relations Careers,* 1988.

Rowh, Mark. *Careers for Crafty People and Other Dexterous Types,* 1993.

———. *Opportunities in Electronics Careers,* 1992.

———. *Opportunities in Waste Management,* 1992.

Sacks, Terry. *Careers in Medicine,* 1993.

Snook, I. Donald, Jr. *Opportunities in Health and Medical Careers,* 1991.

———. *Opportunities in Hospital Administration Careers,* 1989.

Sugar-Webb, Jan. *Opportunities in Physician Careers,* 1991.

Swanson, Barbara. *Careers in Health Care,* 1989.

White, William C. *Opportunities in Agriculture Careers,* 1988.

Wille, Christopher, M. *Opportunities in Forestry Careers,* 1992.

Winter, Charles A. *Opportunities in Biological Science,* 1990.

Wittenberg, Renee. *Opportunities in Social Work Careers,* 1988.

REFERENCE BOOKS

The Handbook of Private Schools: An Annual Descriptive Survey of Independent Education. Boston: Porter Sargent Publishers, Inc., annual. (Lists over 1,750 schools)

Lovejoy's College Guides. New York: Lovejoy's Educational Guides, biannual.

National Trade and Professional Association of the United States. *National Trade and Professional Associations of the United States.* Washington, D.C.: Columbia Books, Inc., annual.

Peterson's Guide to Four-Year Colleges. Princeton, NJ: Peterson's Guides, annual.

Seredich, John, editor. *Your Resource Guide to Environmental Organizations.* Irvine, CA: Smiling Dolphins Press, 1991. (Includes the purposes, programs, accomplishments, opportunities, publications, and membership benefits of 150 environmental organizations)

A complete list of titles in our extensive *Opportunities* series

OPPORTUNITIES IN

Accounting
Acting
Advertising
Aerospace
Airline
Animal & Pet Care
Architecture
Automotive Service
Banking
Beauty Culture
Biological Sciences
Biotechnology
Broadcasting
Building Construction Trades
Business Communication
Business Management
Cable Television
CAD/CAM
Carpentry
Chemistry
Child Care
Chiropractic
Civil Engineering
Cleaning Service
Commercial Art & Graphic
   Design
Computer Maintenance
Computer Science
Counseling & Development
Crafts
Culinary
Customer Service
Data Processing
Dental Care
Desktop Publishing
Direct Marketing
Drafting
Electrical Trades
Electronics
Energy
Engineering
Engineering Technology
Environmental
Eye Care
Farming and Agriculture
Fashion
Fast Food
Federal Government
Film
Financial

Fire Protection Services
Fitness
Food Services
Foreign Language
Forestry
Franchising
Gerontology & Aging Services
Health & Medical
Heating, Ventilation, Air
   Conditioning, and
   Refrigeration
High Tech
Home Economics
Homecare Services
Horticulture
Hospital Administration
Hotel & Motel Management
Human Resource Management
Information Systems
Installation & Repair
Insurance
Interior Design & Decorating
International Business
Journalism
Laser Technology
Law
Law Enforcement & Criminal
   Justice
Library & Information Science
Machine Trades
Marine & Maritime
Marketing
Masonry
Medical Imaging
Medical Technology
Mental Health
Metalworking
Military
Modeling
Music
Nonprofit Organizations
Nursing
Nutrition
Occupational Therapy
Office Occupations
Paralegal
Paramedical
Part-time & Summer Jobs
Performing Arts
Petroleum
Pharmacy
Photography

Physical Therapy
Physician
Physician Assistant
Plastics
Plumbing & Pipe Fitting
Postal Service
Printing
Property Management
Psychology
Public Health
Public Relations
Publishing
Purchasing
Real Estate
Recreation & Leisure
Religious Service
Restaurant
Retailing
Robotics
Sales
Secretarial
Social Science
Social Work
Special Education
Speech-Language Pathology
Sports & Athletics
Sports Medicine
State & Local Government
Teaching
Teaching English to Speakers
   of Other Languages
Technical Writing &
   Communications
Telecommunications
Telemarketing
Television & Video
Theatrical Design &
   Production
Tool & Die
Transportation
Travel
Trucking
Veterinary Medicine
Visual Arts
Vocational & Technical
Warehousing
Waste Management
Welding
Word Processing
Writing
Your Own Service Business

VGM Career Horizons
a division of *NTC Publishing Group*
4255 West Touhy Avenue
Lincolnwood, Illinois 60646–1975